Queen of Executive Suite

Fight for Female Leadership

by
Naomi Walker

Copyright 2024 Lars Meiertoberens. All rights reserved.

No part of this book may be reproduced in any form or by any electronic or mechanical means including information storage and retrieval systems, without permission in writing from the author. The only exception is by a reviewer, who may quote short excerpts in a review.

Although the author and publisher have made every effort to ensure that the information in this book was correct at the time of going to press, the author and publisher accept no liability to any party for any loss, damage or disruption caused by errors or omissions, whether such errors or omissions are due to negligence. accident or any other cause.

This publication is intended to provide accurate and reliable information with respect to the subject matter covered. It is sold on the understanding that the publisher does not provide professional services. If legal advice or other expert assistance is required, the services of a competent professional should be sought.

The fact that an organization or website is mentioned in this work as a citation and/or potential source of further information does not imply that the author or publisher endorses the information the organization or website provides or the recommendations it makes.

Please keep in mind that websites listed in this work may have changed or disappeared between the time this work was written and the time it was read.

Queen of Executive Suite

Fight for Female Leadership

Contents

Introduction: The Rise of the Female Executive 1

Chapter 1: The History of Women in Business 5

Chapter 2: Breaking the Glass Ceiling: Myths and Realities 12

Chapter 3: Leadership Styles: Female vs Male Perspectives 20

Chapter 4: The Power of Mentorship and Networking 28

Chapter 5: Overcoming Bias and Stereotypes 35

Chapter 6: Navigating Work-Life Balance 43

Chapter 7: The Importance of Self-Promotion 50

Chapter 8: The Support System: Family, Friends, and Foes 57

Chapter 9: Strategies for Effective Communication 65

Chapter 10: Decision Making and Risk Taking 73

Chapter 11: Cultivating Executive Presence 81

Chapter 12: Women in Male-Dominated Industries 89

Chapter 13: Tackling the Pay Gap 97

Chapter 14: The Role of Women in Corporate Governance 104

Chapter 15: Entrepreneurship: The Female Vanguard 112

Chapter 16: Embracing Diversity and Inclusion 120

Chapter 17: Technology and Innovation: Women at the Helm 128

Chapter 18: Education and Continuous Learning............................ 135

Chapter 19: Health and Wellness for the Busy Executive 143

Chapter 20: Scaling the Ladder: Promotion Strategies...................... 150

Chapter 21: Coping with Failure and Setbacks 158

Chapter 22: The International Arena: Women
in Global Leadership 166

Chapter 23: Legislation and Policy: The Path to Equality................ 174

Chapter 24: The Future of Female Leadership 182

Chapter 25: An Action Plan for Aspiring Female Leaders................ 190

Chapter 26: The Continuing Quest for Gender Equality in
Leadership... 197

Appendix A: Resources for Female Executives................................. 201

Glossary of Terms.. 204

Appendix B: Interview Transcripts with Female Leaders 208

Introduction:
The Rise of the Female Executive

The landscape of corporate leadership is undergoing an indisputable transformation; a powerful surge is sweeping through the highest echelons of the business world. Gradually yet resolutely, women are carving their niche in this once impenetrable bastion of male dominance. This is not merely about the insertion of a feminine presence in the boardroom but the rise of the female executive — a trailblazer rewriting the narrative of leadership in the 21st century.

The evolution has been slow, marked by formidable challenges and victories hard won. The female leaders of today stand on the shoulders of the indomitable spirits who dared to dream in eras less kind. These pioneers defied societal norms, cultural inhibitions, and financial barricades to grace the marketplace with their unique blend of intelligence, empathy, and resilience. Their journey set the foundation upon which modern women can continue to build, ascending to heights hitherto unreached.

As the pages unfold before you, envision this manuscript as a mirror reflecting the tenacity and spirit of women across the globe. Here lies a narrative steeped in the stories of triumphs over bias, stereotypes, and corporate hurdles. It is a tale that sings praises of women who balance the tightrope of work-life harmony, maintain their health and wellness amidst demanding schedules, and approach decision making with audacity and finesse.

Amidst these triumphs, let us not shy away from acknowledging the complexities that still cloud the journey. The glass ceiling, that invisible yet unyielding barrier, remains a reality for many, as does the disparity in pay and opportunity. While some may debate the existence of this ceiling, the numbers tell a more tangible tale. Nonetheless, it's a tale punctuated by hope and the continual shattering of myths that once stood as irrefutable 'truths'.

Leadership, shaped by an intersection of gendered perspectives, is no longer confined to the aggressive, take-charge archetype that history often records. Instead, it has broadened, merging the strengths of both female and male energies. Women's innate capacity for empathy and collaboration, coupled with strategic risk-taking, presents a dynamic synergy that contemporary businesses cannot afford to overlook.

Acknowledging the value of connections, mentorship and networks have emerged as pivotal elements in the upward mobility of the female executive. The fabric of support woven through allies and mentors is not just about guidance but also about establishing a lattice of empowerment. Family, friends, and even foes, play an instrumental role in shaping the voyage towards leadership excellence.

Furthermore, communication—assertive, impactful and authentic—has become the keystone of women's leadership. The power to articulate one's vision, negotiate one's worth, and command the respect of a room is no longer optional. It's essential. The strategies to amplify one's voice without sacrificing authenticity are what differentiate a leader from a follower.

This narrative is also about breaking grounds in traditionally male-dominated sectors, navigating the complex terrain of corporate governance, and leading companies with innovative fervor. It celebrates the women who have braved the tech frontiers, dominated the entrepreneurial space, and left indelible marks across numerous industries.

For the reader embarking on this journey, the book extends an invitation not just to contemplate the ascent of women in business, but to actively engage in their own path to executive leadership. It bridges the past, present, and future, painting a vivid picture of what has been achieved and the endless possibilities that lie ahead.

What follows is a tapestry of strategies for ascending the career ladder, contending with setbacks, embracing continuous education, and advocating for fair legislation and policies. The diligent pursuit of diversity and inclusion, the challenges and joys of leading within the international scene, and the ongoing struggle for equal representation are all threads within this intricate weave.

Ambitiously, this book aspires not only to narrate the rise of the female executive but to actively participate in it. By laying out an articulate, well-researched, and inspirational roadmap, it serves as a catalyst for the current and next generation of women aiming for the apex of their careers. It's a call to action—encouraging readers to envision their goals, craft their journey, and execute their vision with precision and perseverance.

Let each chapter serve as a counsel, each anecdote as inspiration, and each strategy as a tool for crafting your path to leadership. This is no merely quaint collection of success stories—it's a manual. It's a beacon. It's a declaration that the age of the female executive is not a fleeting moment in the chronicles of business history but a perennial era that is here to stay.

So, take this moment. Absorb the essence of what lies within these pages. Recognize the potential in yourself and in countless other women striving for excellence in leadership. The rise of the female executive is not a quiet dawn. It's a resplendent sunrise, illuminating new pinnacles to conquer and heralding a day where diversity in leadership is not merely aspired to but achieved.

Welcome, then, to a narrative of transformation, empowerment, and leadership through the lens of some of the most formidable players in the corporate sphere: women. It's time to elevate the conversation, alter the game, and continue the ascent. The rise of the female executive is upon us, reshaping the face of leadership one determined step at a time.

Chapter 1:
The History of Women in Business

As the narrative picks up from the evolution highlighted in the introduction, it is essential to delve into the tapestry of history that has seen women emerge from the shadows into the beating heart of the business world. Indeed, the chronicles of women in business are not just stepped in resilience; they are shimmering beacons of progress amidst vast seas of challenges. From the astute business acumen of Elizabeth I to the industrial prowess manifested during the second world war, women have always been an integral, albeit often unrecognised, force in commerce. The quantum leap from cottage industries to boardroom executives did not happen overnight; it has been a relentless march towards economic empowerment and leadership, with women entrepreneurs crafting legacies as robust as any empire. Bearing witness to this history isn't merely an academic exercise but a vital cornerstone for understanding the power and potential that lies within every current and aspiring woman leader. By charting the past milestones and present trends, we ignite the kind of knowledge that does more than inform—it inspires, it mobilises, and it instills the grit needed to shape a future where gender parity is not just envisioned but vigorously achieved.

Past Milestones

In the unfolding narrative of women in business, it is paramount to reflect upon the collective strides and individual triumphs that have charted the course to the present day. The tale of women in corporate leadership is not only about the numbers; it's about the resilience, the breakthroughs, and the bold decisions that shattered perceptions and laid the groundwork for successive generations of female leaders.

The history of women in the business world is, at its core, a testament to tenacity. It begins with incremental advancements, such as in the early 20th century, where women first began to enter the workforce en masse due to exigent circumstances like wars and economic necessity. The valiance displayed during these times is nothing short of inspiring, establishing that women could hold their own in what was traditionally a male-dominated arena.

Post World War II provided new horizons for women as societal norms began to shift, albeit slowly. The 1960s, a period ripe with civil unrest and calls for equality, saw the genesis of the feminist movement, a vital catalyst for change. This era challenged and uprooted deep-seated biases, spurring legislative advancements such as the Equal Pay Act of 1963 in the United States, which aimed to abolish wage disparity based on gender.

As the decades progressed, women not only began to assert their right to equal pay but also started to claim their place in the higher echelons of corporate leadership. The 1970s saw the emergence of female trailblazers who would become the first women to hold executive roles in Fortune 500 companies. These women, undeterred by the status quo, blazed a trail for the leaders of tomorrow.

The 1980s heralded a new chapter with the first woman breaking into the Fortune 500 CEO club, effectively proving that the boardroom was no longer an all-male preserve. Though they were outliers in a world still replete with gender biases, their prominence started to normalise the concept of women at the helm of major enterprises.

By the 1990s, the advancements made were not merely symbolic but were underpinned by a growing body of research that advocated diversity in leadership. It became increasingly evident that companies with women in senior positions showed enhanced performance and governance.

The new millennium brought with it a heightened global consciousness regarding gender parity. The discourse broadened to include not only gender diversity but a comprehensive understanding of women's unique leadership styles and contributions. Networks for supporting women sprang up, recognising the collective strength found in solidarity and shared experiences.

One significant milestone that demonstrated the evolving landscape was the introduction of parental leave policies, tailored to ensure that women did not have to choose between career advancement and family. Acknowledging the importance of work-life balance, such policies began to erode the archaic norm that to succeed in business, one had to sacrifice personal life and well-being.

As the 21st century progressed, we witnessed an inflection point with the formation of global campaigns and initiatives such as the United Nations' HeForShe and Women's Empowerment Principles. These movements laid bare the economic imperatives of gender equality and sought commitments from corporate entities to this end.

Technology, too, became an unexpected equaliser, presenting opportunities for remote work, flexible hours, and novel ways for women to navigate the corporate maze while managing personal commitments. The digital age empowered women with access to information, mentorship, and networks previously out of reach.

Despite the progress, persistent headwinds remained, and in addressing these, institutions began to implement mentorship programs and sponsorships specifically designed for women.

Recognising that role models and guides were crucial in one's ascent, these initiatives worked to close the leadership gap.

Significant, too, were the efforts of women who reached leadership positions and actively worked to lift others. These women leaders understood that their success went hand in hand with a responsibility – to forge an environment that thrives on inclusivity and paves the way for emerging female leaders.

Celebrated moments arrived when stock exchanges around the world started seeing more companies with women in leadership ringing the opening bells, a symbolic gesture, announcing that the corporate world was indeed changing.

Transparency in gender diversity data also became a tool for progress. Companies began to report on the demographic makeup of their leadership teams, bringing accountability and spurring dialogue within and across industries on the importance of gender parity at the decision-making table.

And so, the past milestones, each a building block, have created a foundation upon which the aspirations of today's women are realised. This history is not simply informative; it is dynamic and serves to empower new generations to push even further. It is a story of grit, of pushing boundaries, and of envisioning a world where leadership is defined by capability, not gender. Indeed, the milestones of the past are the stepping stones to a future that reflects true equity across all levels of corporate leadership.

Present Trends

As we acknowledge the strides made by women in the realm of business leadership, it is imperative to examine the currents shaping today's environment. Visible shifts have transformed the corporate landscape, and women now not only aspire to lead but are stepping into leadership roles at an increasing rate.

Contemporary trends speak volumes about progress; more women serve on the boards of major corporations than ever before. Data suggests a gradual, yet positive uptrend in the number of women taking on senior leadership roles. This shift is not just about numbers; it conveys a change in organisational culture and an acknowledgment of the value women bring to the decision-making table.

However, the path isn't bereft of challenges. Women in leadership roles often confront an expectation to strike a delicate balance between assertiveness and approachability, a dichotomy less frequently imposed upon their male counterparts. This phenomenon, while subtly undermining, is being tackled through increased awareness and training programs that aim to cultivate inclusive workplaces.

In terms of sectors, while traditionally feminine industries have historically seen a higher concentration of female leaders, present trends indicate a breach of barriers in more male-dominated fields. The fields of technology, engineering, and finance are witnessing a considerable intake of women who are not just participants, but trailblazers and innovators.

On the entrepreneur front, the surge in women-owned businesses is reshaping the economy. The current era has seen a bevy of successful female entrepreneurs who have created niches for themselves and established robust enterprises. Their impact is far-reaching, setting a precedence for future women leaders and reshaping the entrepreneurial landscape.

Networking is now recognised as a pivotal element of career advancement. Professional networks and mentorship programs specifically catered towards women are burgeoning. These platforms provide women with the access and resources to navigate career advancement, laying the groundwork for a future where women are well-represented in leadership.

The present narrative also encompasses a greater push for transparency around the pay gap. As unease over salary disparities grows, organisations are being compelled to reassess their compensation structures to ensure fairness and equity. This momentum has been aided by the public and legislative calls to action for companies to disclose and address gender pay differences.

Work-life balance, a longstanding concern for many, particularly women, is witnessing an interesting evolution. The concept of flexible working arrangements is gaining traction, championed by the belief that productivity is not solely the result of traditional 9-to-5 workdays. More businesses are recognising the benefits of offering flexibility, thus enabling a more sustainable working model for women juggling multiple roles.

The adoption of diversity and inclusion initiatives has also become a benchmark for corporate progressiveness. Companies are investing in strategies to create more diverse work environments, recognising the business imperative and moral obligation to foster an inclusive culture. These initiatives are no longer just 'nice-to-haves' but critical components of a company's value proposition.

Amidst these positive shifts, a glaring reality persists – the underrepresentation of women in the C-suite. While there has been movement, it's not enough. Recognising this, there is an intensified focus on pipelines that groom women for these top positions, acknowledging the need for deliberate and strategic succession planning that facilitates a more equitable distribution of power.

Another notable trend is the increasing role of social media as a platform for thought leadership. Women are leveraging these channels to build their brands, share insights, and connect with like-minded professionals. This democratisation of voice has provided an unprecedented opportunity for women to influence and inspire far beyond the confines of their immediate networks.

Beyond individual corporate practices, the broader socio-economic context continues to influence the trend of women in leadership. Legislative efforts to require a certain percentage of women in board positions in some countries have started to create mandatory opportunities for women at the highest levels of corporate governance.

Internationally, the discourse on women in leadership transcends borders. Global connections have bolstered the spread of ideas and best practices, facilitating a more united front for tackling gender inequality worldwide. This has enabled a cross-pollination of strategies that are culturally responsive and tailored to drive change in different contexts.

The engagement of men as allies in the journey toward gender equality has also seen more emphasis. The realisation that gender diversity benefits everyone is driving more men to become champions for the cause. Active support from male counterparts in advocating for women's advancement is recognized as a crucial element in driving organisational change.

As we review these present trends, we realise that they are not just fleeting moments but stepping stones towards a more equitable future. The wave of women ascending in leadership is not just about filling quotas or ticking diversity checkboxes; it's about recognising and harnessing the unique value that women bring to the table in driving business success and societal progress.

Chapter 2:
Breaking the Glass Ceiling: Myths and Realities

The glass ceiling—an invisible barrier that holds capable women back from top leadership positions—is often punctuated with myths that perpetuate gender disparities in the corporate sphere. This elusive ceiling isn't simply a metaphor; it's a complex lattice of societal and professional constraints that women navigate daily. Yet, whilst discerning the misconceptions surrounding this barrier, such as the mistaken belief that women lack ambition or the erroneous notion that family commitments invariably trump career aspirations, we uncover the multifaceted truth. The reality is that women are making significant inroads across various industries, embodying resilience and change. This chapter ventures beyond the myths, highlighting the tangible shifts and the inspiring women who have shattered these loftiest layers of corporate stratification. It's about acknowledging the progress made and the work that continues, as we unravel the narrative around the glass ceiling, setting the stage for a deeper exploration of how women are not only confronting but also dismantling these barriers.

Understanding the Metaphor

The concept of the "glass ceiling" has been instrumental in framing the dialogue about gender disparity in the corporate world. It's a metaphor that, while invisible, is painfully palpable for many aspiring and current women leaders. But to tackle the issues that it represents, we must first dissect this metaphor and understand its implications fully.

Imagine an invisible barrier that hovers just above you, allowing you to see the higher echelons of success, yet preventing you from reaching them. This is the essence of what the "glass ceiling" conveys—an unseen yet unbreachable divide that keeps women from ascending to the top ranks of corporate leadership. Its transparency suggests that meritocracy prevails, yet the solidity of the barrier indicates otherwise.

Understanding this metaphor is crucial because it encapsulates the subtleties and complexities of the challenges female professionals face. The glass ceiling isn't about overt discrimination or easily identifiable obstructions. Rather, it's about the systemic, entrenched biases and structural impediments that often go unnoticed and unchallenged.

The "glass ceiling" is not a monolithic barrier; it has multiple layers, each representing different issues such as gender biases, organizational practices, and societal expectations. To shatter this ceiling, one must acknowledge its multifaceted nature and the fact that it stretches beyond the individual to the organizational and societal levels.

One layer of the "glass ceiling" is the entrenched stereotype that leadership embodies traditionally masculine traits. Female leaders often find themselves caught in a double bind where showing assertiveness can be perceived as aggression, whereas displaying empathy may be viewed as a sign of weakness. Understanding how these perceptions contribute to the "glass ceiling" can help in devising strategies to mitigate their effects.

Another aspect of the metaphor pertains to access—or rather, the lack of it—to critical networks and sponsorships. Women are less likely to have powerful sponsors who can advocate for their advancement.

Knowing the underlying reasons can inform the development of networks that foster genuine support for women's progression.

We can't ignore that the "glass ceiling" also symbolizes a lack of role models at the top. If women can't see others like themselves in leadership positions, it's harder for them to envision and carve a path for their own leadership journey. By dissecting this part of the metaphor, we understand the importance of visibility and representation.

The glass ceiling's very invisibility makes it challenging to address. It's insidious in that it often goes unquestioned. Recognizing its existence and bringing it into the spotlight is the first step toward dismantling it. It's about transforming silent acceptance into vocal challenge and dismantling the subtle biases that uphold the ceiling.

Furthermore, the glass ceiling metaphor suggests fragility and the possibility of breakthrough. It's not bulletproof; concerted effort, collective action, and dedicated strategies have pierced it before. Acknowledging this gives hope and a sense of direction for those who feel stifled by its presence.

Moreover, understanding this metaphor allows us to appreciate the incremental cracks that women have already made. Each crack, no matter how small, is progress. It's a testament to the tenacity and resilience of those who have challenged the status quo, paving a slightly smoother path for others to follow.

Comprehending the "glass ceiling" also underscores the importance of policy and legislative changes. When we frame gender inequality as a structural issue rather than an individual problem, it becomes clear that systemic change is necessary. Policies that promote transparency in promotion processes and aim to correct gender imbalance at executive levels are examples of the structural changes needed.

It's also about envisioning a corporate culture that is more inclusive and accommodating. The glass ceiling persists in part due to a prevailing corporate ethos that doesn't fully embrace diversity. Understanding this enables us to ask the right questions about how corporate cultures can evolve to be more nurturing of female leadership.

Lastly, the metaphor of the "glass ceiling" serves as a call-to-arms for solidarity among women. It's a shared experience that can unite women across sectors and hierarchies, fostering a sense of community and mutual support. Collaboration and solidarity are crucial in mobilizing collective power to enact change.

The clarity that comes from understanding the metaphor of the glass ceiling can catalyze a transformative shift in both mindset and action. It's not enough to merely recognize the barrier; there must be an understanding that serves as the foundation for strategic planning and action.

With each informed and intentional effort, the myth of the impenetrable glass ceiling is exposed, and its reality can be altered. It's time to more than just gaze through the translucent divide; it's time to shatter it completely and restructure the architecture of our corporate spheres.

Examining Case Studies

In our pursuit of shattering the often-invisible barrier that separates women from top leadership roles, it's essential to dissect certain narratives—the real-life experiences of women who have forged paths through the corporate tundra. Case studies serve not just as a beacon of what's possible, but as a detailed map that shows us the practical routes and challenges along the journey of female leadership. By delving into these case studies, we aim to harvest valuable insights and lessons that can equip, stimulate, and steer aspiring and existing female leaders within the corporate sphere.

These analyses are not mere stories; they are rigorous examinations of success and failure, reflecting the multifaceted nature of women's experiences in the upper echelons of business. Studying them enables us to observe patterns and distil the essence of what contributes to the rising tide of female executives. Each case becomes a potential blueprint for strategy, an exploration of decision-making under pressure, and a deep dive into the resilience required to succeed in an environment that's not traditionally been welcoming to women.

Linda's emergence in the fintech industry exemplifies the potency of tenacity. Often the only woman in board meetings, she tapped into her expansive knowledge, ensuring a confident voice at the decision-making table. Linda's trajectory shows us the importance of being well-prepared and speaking with authority, even in the face of subtle condescendence or overt challenge.

Equally revealing is the account of Priya, who ascended to the C-suite of a leading pharmaceutical company. Here, mentorship played a pivotal role in her progression. Bolstered by seasoned guidance, Priya not only accelerated her climb but also became a torchbearer for others—demonstrating how mentor-mentee relationships fortify the structure of female advancement in business.

Meanwhile, Fatima's leap into leadership within a manufacturing behemoth is a testament to the might of networking. By forging strategic connections and aligning herself with key influencers, she was able to navigate a traditionally male-dominated industry with acumen and vigour, illuminating a path for others to emulate.

Such stories are rife with techniques for overcoming bias. Consider Sandra, who dismantled stereotypes by delivering unmatched results in a tech giant notorious for its cutthroat competition. Her mastery of data-driven strategy equipped her to challenge the status quo, reshaping perceptions among her peers and superiors.

Then, there's the saga of Joyce, whose balancing act between her executive role and personal life serves as a paragon. Her case underlines the crafting of a harmonious work-life synergy, an undertaking that required both deliberate boundary setting and the pursuit of a supportive corporate culture.

We must pay attention to the subtleties of self-promotion as well, as showcased by Aisha's rise in the ranks of a Fortune 500 company. Aisha's story dissects the art of visibility, demonstrating that self-advocacy is a fine balance between tenacity and tact, a lesson critical for anyone aiming to position themselves for leadership.

The confluence of family support and corporate success is another recurring theme in our case studies. Emily's story highlights how familial backing empowers women leaders to pursue ambitious career goals while contending with societal expectations—an aspect of the female executive's life that can't be overlooked.

Effective communication, often the bulwark of leadership, finds resonance in tales such as Naomi's. As she broke through to the helm of a global consultancy firm, her assertiveness combined with empathy, serves as a study in feminine leadership communication styles that break barriers and build bridges.

Risk-taking, too, emerges as a defining feature, as illustrated by Hannah's ascent in the investment banking sector. Her willingness to make bold moves, backed by astute judgement and calculated risk-taking, aligns with our understanding that leadership often entails stepping outside the circle of comfort to achieve greatness.

Executive presence, a nebulous but powerful construct, is epitomised by Laura's influence in an advertising empire. Her case unpacks the elements of gravitas and authority, challenging the misconception that these are inherently male attributes and proving that women can craft a commanding presence without compromising authenticity.

Our exploration would be lacking if we didn't consider women in male-dominated domains. Jessica's pioneering in aerospace—a field fraught with gender imbalance – offers a microscopic view of grit and determination that thrusts barriers aside, spotlighting the industry-specific challenges and strategies for succeeding against the odds.

The compensation conundrum is laid bare in stories such as that of Elizabeth, who, through diligent research and skilful negotiation, tackled the insidious pay gap issue head-on, revealing tactics from which every woman can learn in their quest for equitable remuneration.

In the broader canopy of corporate governance, Angela's experience on the board of an international oil conglomerate reflects the intrinsic value of board diversity. Her ability to influence policy and shape a culture of inclusivity creates ripples that extend far beyond her individual role.

These case studies, each a repository of wisdom, cement the fact that theories and abstract notions of empowerment only go so far without the foundation of real-life examples. As women seeking a revolution in the composition of leadership, these stories are not just inspiration—they are invaluable resources. The mosaic of female corporate leadership unfolds before us, rich with complexity, challenge, and triumph, painting a picture that is both instructive and heartening for the road ahead.

Empowered with these insights, we can now forge ahead with greater clarity and determination. As women in pursuit of exemplary leadership roles, we are not starting from scratch. We stand on the shoulders of those who have navigated these peaks and valleys before us. Each case study is a torch in the long night of gender disparity—a burning testament to what we can achieve and how we might navigate our own careers in the journey toward corporate equity and leadership excellence.

Chapter 3:
Leadership Styles: Female vs Male Perspectives

As we delve into the complex tapestry of leadership, an understanding of how men and women typically navigate their executive roles is pivotal. The intricacies of leadership styles from female versus male perspectives reveal patterns that, while not absolute, provide insight into a gender-influenced dynamic. Notably, women's leadership often embodies transformational qualities, fostering collaboration, empathy, and inclusivity, an approach that empowers teams and encourages shared success. In contrast, traditional male leadership has gravitated towards a transactional style, highlighting the power of authority, decisiveness, and competition. It's crucial, however, to avoid overgeneralisations in this comparison; the most effective leaders typically display a blend of these attributes, irrespective of gender. This chapter aims to dissect these perspectives, offering strategies to harness the best of both worlds, enabling female leaders to redefine success within the corporate paradigm, by leveraging the inherent strengths found across the leadership spectrum.

Mapping the Differences

As we pivot from discussing leadership styles in general, we approach a vital juncture—the discernible contrasts between male and female leadership approaches. While gender should not predicate the quality or style of leadership, it's undeniable that social conditioning and cultural expectations can influence how leaders operate within corporate environments. Knowledge of these nuanced differences is crucial for understanding, appreciating, and leveraging the unique attributes women bring to the forefront of business leadership.

Historically, male leaders have often been associated with traits like decisiveness, assertiveness, and a command-and-control style of governance. These attributes have served male-dominated industries well, fitting snugly into the ethos of competitive business landscapes. The archetype of a forceful executive, leading with an iron fist and an undeterred focus on results, prevails in collective corporate consciousness.

Female leadership, by contrast, often embodies a different set of qualities—ones that foster collaboration, empathy, and inclusivity. Women leaders tend to nurture a working environment where team members can thrive and encourage open communication and shared responsibility. This style is not indicative of being 'soft' or less determined but represents a redefinition of strength—a strength characterised by resilience, adaptability, and understanding the human side of the business equation.

These distinct leadership fingerprints are not just theoretical musings; they're backed by research and observable outcomes. Studies have shown that female executives excel in areas of emotional intelligence, such as social awareness and self-awareness, which are critical for managing dynamics within teams and aligning diverse groups behind a common mission.

Take the concept of transformational leadership, for instance, where the focus is on inspiring and motivating employees rather than dictating orders. Women's propensity for this model of leadership can be particularly effective in today's fast-paced and constantly evolving corporate milieu. The ability to galvanise a team, drive innovation through shared visioning, and lead by example, translates into tangible business successes.

However, it's imperative to avoid falling into the trap of binary thinking or overgeneralisation. Not all women, nor men, will fit neatly into these described paradigms. Personalities, experiences, and situational contexts also play significant roles in shaping leadership styles. Thus, while we map the differences, it's equally important to honour the spectrum of personal leadership approaches that individuals, irrespective of gender, bring to the table.

In discussing these differences, one must consider the concept of situational leadership, where adaptability is key. In certain contexts, a directive approach might be necessary—such as during crises, when quick and decisive action is required. Women are equally capable of this form of leadership, although they may not be as readily associated with it. The versatility in switching between leadership styles is an asset that female leaders often possess and one which serves companies well in turbulent times.

As we progress through this journey of recognition and appreciation, let's also spotlight the important role of communication styles. Women tend to use communication as a tool for relationship-building and problem-solving, often favouring a cooperative rather than a competitive approach. This method allows for a more democratic and inclusive decision-making process, where the insights and opinions of team members are valued and considered.

In the realm of decision-making, there's an intriguing divergence to consider. Women leaders tend to be more deliberate and consultative, seeking a broad range of perspectives before arriving at a conclusion. This thoroughness should be viewed as an asset rather than a hindrance to swift action. It reflects a meticulous and holistic view of the business landscape, considering the repercussions of decisions not only on the balance sheet but also on people and long-term strategy.

This consultative approach should not, however, be misconstrued as indecisiveness or lack of confidence. Rather, it's an acknowledgement that in the complex world of business, the best decisions often stem from collective insight. This can lead to more sustainable success and a positive workplace culture that champions shared achievements.

Another critical difference is the approach to risk. While courage and boldness are not the sole province of any gender, female leaders often demonstrate a more calculated approach to risk. This can result in more stable and consistent performance over time, rather than the potentially erratic outcomes of high-risk strategies.

As we chart these nuanced variances, it's also noteworthy to mention how women in leadership roles can impact corporate social responsibility (CSR) and ethical practices. The inclination towards ethical leadership, with attention to social and environmental impacts, is an area where women have notably made a difference, fostering trust and loyalty among stakeholders.

Innovation is yet another frontier where women are carving a distinct path. Female leaders often approach innovation collaboratively and with an emphasis on diverse inputs, leading to unique and breakthrough ideas. Their focus on inclusive innovation can create an ecosystem where creativity flourishes beyond the conventional bounds set by a homogenous leadership composition.

Understanding and embracing these differences provides a foundation for developing a multifaceted leadership model. One that combines the strengths inherent in both female and male leadership styles can reshape an organisation's strategic direction towards a more diverse, resilient, and inclusive future.

In summation, while the corporate leadership landscape may have been historically one-dimensional, the rise of female executives is painting a new picture of effective leadership. It's a rich tapestry threaded with care, collaboration, and innovative perspectives. By recognising and celebrating these differences, we could not only redefine leadership excellence but also drive businesses towards a more equitable, ethical, and profitable era.

Blending the Strengths

As we delve into the complexities of leadership, it becomes clear that the ingenuity of an organisation often springs from the harmonic blending of diverse strengths. In a world where leadership traits are not the exclusive domain of one gender, women leaders bring a plethora of abilities and perspectives that when combined with male counterparts, can lead to an enriched leadership tapestry catalysing innovation and efficiency within the workplace.

Analyzing leadership styles has revealed that women often exhibit transformational leadership qualities, such as empathy, effective communication, and a collaborative approach. These strengths, inherently valuable, become even more potent when integrated with the more traditional, command-and-control leadership styles that some male leaders portray. The confluence of these styles sparks a synergy that can drive teams towards exceptional performance.

Consider the power of empathy in leadership, a trait strongly associated with female leaders. Empathy allows leaders to connect with their staff on a deeper level, fostering an environment of trust and mutual respect. When men and women in leadership supplement this with strategic decision-making, often highlighted as a male strength, organisations can benefit from leaders who are not only decisive but also deeply cognizant of the morale and well-being of their teams.

Effective communication is another arena where the blending of male and female leadership strengths can be transformative. Inclusive communication, commonly practised by women, when combined with assertive and directive communication, seen more frequently in their male counterparts, leads to messages that are both empowering and clarifying, ensuring that no member of the team feels left behind or misunderstood.

In the realm of collaboration, women often excel, promoting an environment where ideas are shared freely and team members are encouraged to contribute. When this is paired with the results-driven focus that is a hallmark of many male leaders, the result is a team that not only generates a broad spectrum of ideas but is also adept at implementing these ideas effectively to achieve goals.

Moreover, the integration of different leadership strengths creates a fertile ground for innovation. The fresh perspectives offered by women, coupled with the analytical and risk-taking approaches that men often exhibit, can result in pioneering solutions and groundbreaking business strategies that keep companies at the forefront of their industries.

It is also vital to acknowledge the role of emotional intelligence in leadership – an area where female leaders often excel. This intelligence, when paired with the confidence and courage typically associated with male leadership, equips teams with the ability to navigate corporate landscapes with both intuition and fearlessness.

Furthermore, when women blend their typically strong interpersonal skills with the delegative prowess that male leaders may exhibit, organisations can experience a balance of nurturing talent while also driving accountability. This serves to build a strong workforce that feels valued and is clear on expectations and responsibilities.

Risk management is yet another area that benefits from gender-inclusive leadership. Women tend to be more risk-aware and consider a broader range of factors in decision-making, which can mitigate potential pitfalls. Men's propensity to be more risk-tolerant can energize an organisation to pursue bold ventures. Together, these approaches create a well-rounded risk management strategy.

Inclusion is the cornerstone of the blended approach, with women often championing diversity and inclusivity in leadership. When this inclusivity is combined with the typically more hierarchical structures men might maintain, a unique leadership framework emerges that values individual contributions while providing clear directional guidance – an essential dynamic for large-scale organisations.

It is important to highlight the concept of shared leadership, where the strengths of individual team members are recognized and utilized. This is an area where female leaders often thrive, promoting a shared sense of responsibility and ownership. When this approach is coupled with the directional clarity that male leaders can provide, it strengthens the collective capacity for leadership within the team.

Negotiation skills are also enhanced in a gender-inclusive leadership environment. The integrative negotiation style that women often adopt, which looks for win-win solutions, complements the more competitive style of men, leading to negotiations that accommodate the needs of all parties while also driving hard bargains when necessary.

One cannot overlook the role of nurturing talent and leadership development as critical elements of effective leadership. Women leaders are often seen as coaches and mentors, investing in the growth of their team members. When combined with the more performance-focused approach that many men take, it provides a balanced growth environment for employees, driving both personal development and business results.

Strategic vision, often a strength of male leaders, when interwoven with the holistic and long-term visions that women bring to the table, creates comprehensive strategic plans that are both ambitious and attentive to the intricacies of the business landscape.

Last but not least, resilience, a trait embodied by many women who have navigated through gender biases to reach leadership positions, when joined with the competitiveness often seen in male leaders, forms a leadership front that is both hardy and driven, essential for any organisation looking to sustain itself and thrive in an ever-changing world.

Blending the strengths of male and female leadership styles is not just beneficial; it is imperative for organisations that aspire to stay relevant and successful in today's global and highly nuanced market. Leaders who embrace and combine the complementing skills and approaches that each gender offers, amplify the potential for success, catalyzing a work environment that is dynamic, just, and productive.

Chapter 4:
The Power of Mentorship and Networking

The ascent to leadership is seldom a solitary climb; it thrives on the support of robust scaffolding built around the power of mentorship and networking. Within the intricate dance of professional development, finding a mentor is akin to discovering an invaluable compass—one that guides through treacherous terrains of corporate intricacies with the insights of experienced navigation. It's the sharing of wisdom that turns potential pitfalls into stepping stones towards success. Networking, in its essence, is the art of cultivating connections, weaving a tapestry of relationships that can uplift, endorse, and propel one's career forward. It's an investment of time and energy in a community that reciprocates with opportunities and empowerment. For women in leadership, these dynamic interplays are not just advantageous; they are critical. They have the capacity to wield a transformative influence—an alchemy that converts individual aspirations into collective achievements, shaping the corporate landscape with each new connection forged and every piece of insight gained.

Finding a Mentor

The journey to the apex of any career, especially in the challenging terrains of corporate leadership, warrants not just sheer will and aptitude but guided expertise. A mentor serves this crucial role, offering a compass in a labyrinth where gender-based obstacles abound. Finding a mentor is a deliberate and pivotal step, demanding strategy and sincere commitment. It is not merely about seeking advice but forging a relationship pivotal to professional and personal growth. Here, we explore the nuances of finding that guiding star—someone who will challenge and champion you.

To initiate the search for a mentor, start with a clear acknowledgement of your goals. Reflect on where you stand, what you aspire to achieve, and the kind of leadership qualities you wish to embody. Articulation of these elements not only crystallises your vision but also aids in pinpointing a mentor whose expertise and career trajectory resonate with your objectives.

Once your goals are defined, the next step is to survey your existing network. Often, a potential mentor may already be within your circle, be it a senior professional in your organization or an industry connection you've made at a conference. If there's nobody immediately apparent, widen your scope. Seek out industry events, join relevant groups and forums online, and establish connections with figures you admire from afar. Remember, a mentor does not necessarily need to be a female, although shared gender experiences can enrich the mentor-mentee relationship.

After identifying potential mentors, approach them with respect for their time and accomplishments. Reach out through a well-crafted message that conveys your admiration for their work and your desire to learn from them. Be specific about what you seek from the mentorship and how you believe they can assist you. This demonstrates your seriousness and that you've done your due diligence.

When you secure an initial meeting, prepare meticulously. Research your prospective mentor's career, understand their contributions, and have a list of thoughtful questions. This meeting is not simply an interview but a two-way discourse that sets the foundation of your mentor-mentee relationship.

Recognise the importance of professional chemistry in this potential relationship. It should feel natural, a mutual understanding and respect fostered over interactions. You can't force a connection; it's about finding someone who genuinely believes in your potential and is excited about nurturing your growth.

Should a mentorship offer come to fruition, set clear expectations from the outset. Engage in an open dialogue about the frequency of meetings, the form of communication preferred, and the feedback mechanisms that will guide your interactions. Transparent conversations like this set the groundwork for a successful mentor-mentee alliance.

It's imperative to note that mentorship is not a one-way street. You must bring value to the table as well. This can be in the form of your unique perspectives, reciprocal help, or even keeping your mentor abreast with fresh ideas and industry trends. This dynamic deepens the relationship, creating a symbiotic bond.

Demonstrate your commitment to the relationship by acting on the guidance provided. Apply lessons learnt, show progress, and keep your mentor updated on your achievements as well as your setbacks. How you implement advice and bounce back from challenges is as telling as your successes.

Should the mentorship face hurdles, such as differences in opinion or directions, address them with professionalism and poise. It's important to maintain respect for your mentor's expertise while also being true to your personal values and vision.

In the instance you seek multiple mentors, which is often advisable to garner a variety of perspectives, ensure each relationship is given its due diligence. The mosaic of advice will only be beneficial if you are able to integrate it effectively within your personal style and objectives.

Remember, the goal of mentorship is not just about climbing the ladder more swiftly; it should enrich you with profound insights and skills that last a lifetime. Focus not just on the destination but also on the breadth and depth of your journey. A mentor can infuse your path with wisdom that illuminates the way forward and inward.

As your career progresses, you may inevitably outgrow the mentorship, or rather, evolve from it. This is a natural, often positive outcome of successful mentor relationships. Always conclude these chapters with gratitude and maintain connections, for the networks you forge can serve you in ways you may not anticipate.

Finally, as you advance, pay forward the mentorship you've received. Becoming a mentor yourself not only contributes to the cycle of empowerment but also offers you a refreshed perspective on your own journey. You'll find that teaching often informs the teacher as much as the student.

Indeed, finding a mentor is an evolution in practice. It is a testament to the strength of collaboration over competition. It signifies a willingness to not only ascend within the hierarchical constructs of corporate business but to do so with grace, wisdom, and the cumulative knowledge of those who have navigated these realms before us. Embrace the search for a mentor as you do your own professional pursuit with poise, patience, and unyielding perseverance.

Building Your Network

As we advance in the chapters, it becomes increasingly obvious that a strong network is not just a safety net; it is an essential ladder to reach heights in your career that might otherwise be inaccessible. For women in leadership, a robust and diverse network is vital to breaking through barriers, both seen and unseen. This network extends far beyond collecting business cards and adding connections on LinkedIn. It's about forging relationships that are both meaningful and mutually beneficial.

The notion of networking can evoke images of formal corporate events, yet the reality is that opportunities for connection are woven into the fabric of our daily lives. The commencement of building a network starts with recognising the value in every interaction – be it at a conference, through a volunteer activity, or within the office. It pays to have a strategic approach, understanding that a well-curated network brings a breadth of perspectives, skills, and opportunities.

A first step to broadening your professional network is to step outside the comfort zone of your immediate circle. Attend industry conferences, engage with online professional groups, and don't hesitate to strike up conversations. In each interaction lies a potential long-term professional relationship. Diversifying your contacts by industry, seniority, and background can expose you to different viewpoints and opportunities, cultivating a rich professional tapestry.

Maintaining these connections is equally as important as creating them. A simple follow-up email after an event expressing your interest in keeping in touch, or sharing an article relevant to a discussion you had can make all the difference. It communicates that you value the connection and are invested in nurturing it. Remember, networking is a two-way street where the value of give and take can't be underestimated.

Investing time in professional associations can also be a game-changer. These organisations are not just about attending meetings; they're a direct line to industry knowledge and a hub for like-minded professionals. It's a platform where you can share your own knowledge, too – perhaps through speaking engagements or panel discussions, which in turn can elevate your visibility and authority in your field.

Social media platforms, when used strategically, are potent networking tools. They provide a space to showcase your expertise, share insights, and engage with the thoughts of others. This can often lead to meaningful offline interactions. However, your digital engagement should be thoughtful, cultivating a personal brand that aligns with your career aspirations.

Peer networks often go overlooked, but they can be one of the most supportive environments for professional growth. Cultivate relationships with your counterparts. These are people who understand your challenges and can offer insights and support as you navigate your career. It can be empowering to grow alongside your peers, celebrating successes and learning from one another's experiences.

Networking within your own organisation can also unlock doors. Taking interest in cross-departmental projects or joining internal committees can expose you to new areas of the business and new people. It showcases your initiative and willingness to take on new challenges, which can be noticed by those in leadership positions.

Making the transition from a network to a sponsorship can take your career to the next level. Sponsors, who are typically in higher positions of power, do more than offer advice; they advocate for you. Forming relationships with individuals who have the influence to propel your career forward is critical. They can open doors to opportunities and endorse you for roles or projects that you might not have access to otherwise.

Remember, networking is not a short-term investment; it's a lifelong commitment. The seeds you plant today may bear fruit in days, months, or even years to come. It's essential to continuously invest in these relationships, not only when you need help or are looking for the next opportunity. Supporting others in their time of need can strengthen your connections significantly.

Feedback and reflection are often undervalued aspects of networking. Seek feedback from your network not just about potential opportunities, but on your ideas and strategies. It's a great way to gain different perspectives that can help you refine your approach. Reflect on the feedback and take actionable steps to improve or adjust your strategies.

Finally, remember that networking is as much about personal growth as it is about professional advancement. Each person you meet has something unique to teach you, and every interaction has the potential to influence your path. Embrace the learning opportunities that come with networking, as they can shape not only your career but also your personal development.

Building a strong network requires consistent effort, strategic thinking, and authenticity. It's about mutual support and respect, being open to diverse perspectives, and investing in relationships. In the journey to leadership, a solid network is not just an asset, it's an imperative tool for success, opening doors and providing support through the inevitable challenges. Remember, the art of networking is an invaluable skill that, when mastered, facilitates not only your progress but also contributes to reshaping the corporate landscape into a more diverse and vibrant ecosystem.

As we weave our way through the complexities of professional relationships, it is crucial to retain a sense of self while being adaptable in our approach. Your network is a reflection of who you are as a professional, and cultivating it with care is one of the many strides towards a future where leadership is enhanced through diversity, inclusion, and an unwavering commitment to growth.

Chapter 5:
Overcoming Bias and Stereotypes

In the journey towards equitable leadership, recognising and dismantling the barriers of bias and stereotypes stands as a quintessential stride. Evolved as a protective heuristic, bias can, unfortunately, reinforce gender stereotypes and anchor women to dated perceptions in the workplace. However, it's essential to note that cultivating awareness is the first step in a calculated march against these invisible enemies. As aspirants and stewards of change, women can employ an array of strategies to subvert prejudiced views and rewrite the narrative. This chapter delves into not just the identification of common misconceptions but also arms you with practical countermeasures, ensuring that actions and choices echo a commitment to equality. Through understanding and proactive confrontation, we dispel the shadows cast by biases, allowing talent and tenacity to radiate unimpeded in the corporate realm.

Identifying Common Prejudices

In the pursuit of gender equality within the corporate realm, it becomes vital to address a pivotal barrier faced by many: prejudice. Though we have made strides in acknowledging the existence of biases, recognising the nuanced prejudices that pervade the workplace is essential for dismantling them. Within this chapter, we shall delve into the common misconceptions and preconceived notions that often hamstring the advancement of female professionals in the business landscape.

Prejudices often stem from implicit biases—those unconscious beliefs that influence our decisions and behaviour without us being aware of them. These can manifest as a subtle inclination to favour a candidate who seems familiar, or a discomfort with those who do not fit the traditional mould of leadership. While grappling with these biases, it's crucial to consider their many incarnations, from the assumption that women are less committed if they have family responsibilities, to the stereotype that they lack the necessary assertiveness for leadership roles.

Another prevalent stereotype is the myth of the 'emotional' female leader, which perpetuates the notion that women are governed by their feelings and thus, unfit to make tough decisions. This prejudicial belief fails to recognise that emotional intelligence is a strength that can enhance leadership, allowing for greater empathy and understanding in a team dynamic.

Gendered expectations around communication styles also lead to unfair judgments. Women's assertiveness can quickly be misconstrued as aggressiveness, whereas a quieter demeanour might be mistaken for passivity or a lack of confidence. These narrow definitions of acceptable behaviour trap female leaders in a paradoxical standard where it's challenging to strike the appropriate balance that is seldom expected of their male counterparts.

In the same vein of communication, social biases regarding language also present unique hurdles. Women are frequently criticised for employing 'up-talk' or 'vocal fry', speech patterns that, though inconsequential to their capability, can be seized upon to undermine their authority. This focus on how women speak rather than what they are saying is a subtle yet significant impediment to their advancement.

The notion of male incumbency in certain roles also casts long shadows of prejudice, making the climb arduous for women in male-dominated industries. These prejudices can take the form of questions about a woman's technical expertise, physical stamina, or strategic vision. Challenging these stereotypes involves not only acknowledging the credibility of women in these areas but also amplifying their success stories to cultivate a new narrative.

Expectations about appearance also inject prejudice into the professional environment. Women often encounter a double-edged sword where their appearance is scrutinised to a degree not applied to men. The decision to present oneself in a manner that feels authentic can clash with archaic corporate expectations of femininity or professionalism.

Ingrained prejudices seep into evaluative processes as well, affecting performance reviews and promotions. The same achievements may be framed differently based on the gender of the achiever, with women's successes sometimes attributed to luck or the assistance of others, rather than to skill or determination. This undermines meritocracy, depriving talented female leaders of the recognition and opportunities they deserve.

Another deep-seated prejudice is the 'motherhood penalty', which assumes career interruptions or reduced commitment from women with children. Countering this requires a shift in perspective to see parental leave, whether for mothers or fathers, as a natural part of a well-rounded professional life.

The bias of 'likeability' places women in a precarious position where their professional competency might be negatively correlated with their perceived friendliness. Women who assert their authority risk being labelled as less likeable, complicating their career trajectory with an unreasonable demand to be both highly capable and perpetually pleasant.

Within the global corporate setting, prejudices can intersect with cultural stereotypes, creating a multidimensional maze for women to navigate. Female executives from diverse backgrounds might encounter biases that compound gender with ethnicity, accentuating the difficulty of establishing themselves as leaders.

Prejudice can also manifest in the form of networking opportunities, where informal 'boys' clubs' exclude women from crucial relationship-building events. Overcoming this bias means creating inclusive networks that acknowledge the value of diverse connections, and encourage the exchange of ideas across gender lines.

We must also consider the role of media representation in shaping prejudices. Stereotypical portrayals of women in leadership positions can either reinforce dated biases or help break them down. By promoting media that showcases female leaders in a nuanced and positive light, society can begin to inherently question and ultimately discard the harmful stereotypes that have persisted.

To truly identify the prejudices female leaders face requires a constant process of reflection and action—both individually and institutionally. It's about perceiving the attitudinal nuances and systemic structures that, when left unchecked, perpetuate gender imbalances. Recognising these biases represents the first step toward crafting interventions tailored to eliminate them from the workplace.

Ultimately, as aspiring or established female leaders, to grasp prejudices fully is to be armed against them. It's to prepare oneself to deftly navigate the labyrinth of corporate culture, armed with the knowledge and resolve to not only reach but redefine the heights of leadership. We must encourage mentorship, foster open discussions about biases, and actively promote policies and practices that support gender equality. Only then can we claim to create not just a fairer workplace, but a more effective, more humane one.

Strategies for Counteraction

Combatting bias and stereotypes requires a multifaceted approach, one that blends awareness, action, and advocacy. As we delve into strategies for counteraction, let's recall the history of women in business and the progress made thus far. Those past milestones lay the groundwork for developing tactics to dismantle the current prejudices that still hinder many women aspiring to leadership.

Firstly, it's essential to acknowledge that the domain of leadership does not exist separate from societal norms and cultural influences. Unconscious biases, those deep-seated prejudices we harbour without conscious awareness, are one of the most prevalent barriers faced in the workplace. To counteract these biases, awareness is pivotal. Companies can employ training programs designed to make individuals consciously aware of their biases. While awareness alone may not eliminate prejudice, it is the critical first step toward behavioural change.

Another powerful countermeasure is institutional policy change. Organisations that set transparent criteria for hiring and promotions help to curtail the influence of stereotypes. Performance evaluations should be standardised and regularly audited for bias, ensuring that meritocracy prevails over preconceived notions related to gender. Clear-cut policies prevent ambiguity, which often serves as a breeding ground for bias.

Furthermore, mentorship plays a key role in equipping women with the tools required to navigate and dismantle stereotypes. When established leaders take on the responsibility of mentoring emerging female talent, they not only guide them through the intricacies of career advancement but also demonstrate by example how to overcome gender barriers.

Networking, while often touted in business contexts, is essential when it comes to counteracting challenges specific to women. By building a robust professional network, women can support and bolster one another's esteem, share strategic insights, and unlock opportunities that might otherwise be clouded by gender biases.

Initiating open dialogue about gender stereotypes in the workplace is another strategy to combat them. When leaders foster environments where such conversations can take place without fear of repercussions, it brings awareness and encourages collective problem-solving. Inclusivity councils or diversity committees within organisations can be powerful platforms for such dialogs.

Role modelling is an underappreciated yet potent strategy. When women are seen in leadership positions, it challenges the stereotype of leadership being a male domain. This visibility alters perceptions and inspires other women to aspire to such roles, fostering a culture that genuinely recognises and values women's leadership contributions.

Organisations benefit from implementing formal sponsorship programs where executives are tasked with actively promoting the careers of talented women. Unlike mentors, sponsors not only advise but also advocate for their protégés, ensuring that women's accomplishments are recognised and rewarded – a crucial step in breaking the cycle of invisibility that many women face.

Personal branding comes to the forefront as an individual strategy. Women need to project their executive presence by building a compelling personal brand that showcases their unique strengths and leadership attributes. By actively managing how they are perceived within the professional domain, women can take control of their narrative, positioning themselves as capable leaders.

Never underestimate the power of knowledge and continuous self-improvement. Women leaders should be committed to expanding their expertise and skillset, which adds credibility and can offset biases by shifting the focus to proven competence and tangible results.

Assertive communication is another tool in the arsenal against stereotypes. Women need to voice their opinions clearly and confidently, thus dispelling the myth that women are less decisive or assertive than their male counterparts. Mastering the art of assertiveness without crossing into perceived aggressiveness is a delicate but vital skill.

Negotiation skills are also crucial. Whether advocating for a project, negotiating salaries, or pitching for a promotion, being adept in negotiation can help women to assert their value and push back against undervaluation, a common result of gender stereotypes.

Leading by example is perhaps one of the most powerful strategies. When women in leadership positions embody ethical conduct, professionalism, and competence, they redefine norms and expectations, paving the way for other women and influencing the organisational culture.

The introduction of flexible working arrangements can also play a significant role in counteracting bias. By normalising flexible working hours and remote work, organisations can help dismantle the stereotype that ambitious professional women must choose between career success and a fulfilling personal or family life.

Lastly, societal change is fueled by advocacy and policy reform. Women leaders should utilise their platform to champion legislative changes that support gender equality, parental leave, and anti-discrimination laws. This not only benefits the individual leader but also creates a ripple effect benefiting future generations.

In sum, counteracting bias and stereotypes necessitates a blend of personal empowerment and systemic change. By cultivating self-awareness, building robust networks, and fostering organisational cultures that value diversity, we can create an environment where the glass ceiling is not just cracked but dismantled entirely. As we march towards a more inclusive leadership future, our collective action can lead to sustainable impact – promoting a corporate landscape that not only accepts but celebrates female leadership.

Chapter 6:
Navigating Work-Life Balance

Upon shattering the proverbial glass ceiling and stepping into the limelight of leadership, the conundrum of maintaining equilibrium in one's professional and personal spheres becomes more pressing than ever. In this chapter, we'll explore how women can cultivate a work-life harmony that resonates with their individual values and career ambitions. It's about crafting a symphony where the melodies of career success and personal fulfilment complement rather than compete. Through pragmatic tips and real-world examples, we'll delve into how you can set boundaries without stifling progress, and prioritise without apology. Our discourse will navigate through seasons of sacrifice and bounty, with the acknowledgment that balance is not a destination but a dynamic, ever-evolving journey. Join us as we chart a course through the challenges and elucidate the strategies that enable female leaders to thrive amidst the ebb and flow of their multifaceted roles.

Creating Your Harmony

As we delve into the complexities of navigating work-life balance, we must strive towards the concept of creating harmony - a bespoke melding of professional ambitions with personal fulfilment. It's essential to recognise that harmonising these elements is not about achieving a perfect balance per se, but rather about cultivating an environment where one's career and life outside of work can coexist in a mutually supportive manner.

To initiate this process, one must first delineate one's values and practices. It's not enough to have goals in both spheres; they must be interconnected and mutually reinforcing. The harmony we seek is facilitated by a clear understanding of what truly matters for us, which in turn can guide our decisions and actions.

Setting boundaries is another pivotal step. In today's always-connected world, it's too easy to let work encroach upon our personal time and vice versa. We must be resolute in protecting our time and respectful of the lines we draw. This not only helps with managing our own well-being but also sets a healthy example for our colleagues and teams.

A crucial aspect of achieving harmony is mastering the art of delegation. A leader empowers her team, trusting them with responsibilities, which in turn frees her up to focus on tasks that merit her expertise. This approach requires relinquishing some control—a challenge for many—but in doing so, it boosts team confidence and effectiveness.

Time management takes on a new significance when creating harmony. Prioritising tasks, eliminating time-wasters, and even small adjustments like optimising email-reading times can make a substantive difference. It's not just about working smarter; it's about carving out undisturbed time for life's other passions and responsibilities.

Technology, while often a culprit of imbalance, can also be a harbinger of harmony when used judiciously. The judicious implementation of productivity apps, communication tools, and digital calendars can coalesce our diverse responsibilities into a manageable flow, allowing us to oversee our complex lives with greater ease.

Fostering a support network is a linchpin in this dialogue. This ecosystem should comprise individuals who bolster both your career and personal life, including mentors, peers, friends, and family. Their insight and encouragement can be a source of strength and a reminder of the multifaceted nature of your world.

Moreover, self-care must be non-negotiable. A leader cannot pour from an empty cup. Ensuring that there is time for self-replenishment—be it through exercise, meditation, hobbies, or rest—is as critical as any business meeting. Self-care isn't an indulgence; it's a strategic imperative for sustained productivity and health.

While discussing harmony, one cannot overlook the impact of a supportive workplace culture. Organisations play a significant part in how effectively individuals can align their career with their personal lives. Flexible work arrangements, parental leave policies, and a culture that values employee well-being all contribute to this equation.

If we are to lead by example, embracing authenticity is essential. It's empowering to openly discuss the challenges and strategies around work-life harmony with your team. This transparency can inspire others to pursue their own equilibrium and advocate for a culture that prioritises balanced living.

For women in leadership, the matter of harmony often intersects with gender expectations. It's vital to challenge these norms and champion a landscape where women's career progress isn't unfairly tethered to their role within the home. Redefining success on our terms can dismantle antiquated paradigms.

Through the lens of parenthood, creating harmony can be uniquely challenging. The evolution into motherhood adds a glorious, yet intricate, layer to life. It's a period where flexibility, support, and a commitment to one's professional ethos become even more profound. It's a time for recalibrating, not retreating.

Cultivating resilience is intrinsically linked with this pursuit of harmony. Setbacks will occur—unanticipated demands on our time and energy that disrupt the balance we seek. The fortitude to persist and readjust, without succumbing to self-doubt or external pressures, is a testament to one's leadership.

Integrating mindfulness practices can also be a strategic tool in the creation of harmony. Mindfulness encourages presence and focus, qualities that are invaluable when managing the multifaceted needs of one's life. It's about being present in the moment, whether in the boardroom or at the dinner table.

In summary, the creation of your harmony is an ongoing, dynamic process. It necessitates a blend of introspection and action, advocacy and adaptability. It involves setting a precedent—not just for personal achievement, but for the nourishment of a culture wherein the thriving of women in leadership is the norm, not the exception. In stitching together the disparate parts of our lives into a cohesive whole, we define and refine the essence of who we are, and who we aspire to be, both as leaders and individuals.

Case Studies of Successful Balances

It is imperative, as we navigate the complexities of work-life balance, to shed light on authentic narratives of those who have mastered this equilibrium. The following case studies demonstrate how successful women have redefined the boundaries between their careers and personal lives, crafting unique solutions that align with their values, responsibilities, and aspirations.

Consider Natalie, a high-flying investment banker who reached the apex of her career while nurturing a family of three children. Natalie initiated a conversation with her employers about flexible working hours and worked out a plan that allowed her to start her day earlier and leave in time to pick her children up from school. She then logged back on in the evening, if necessary. Her productivity maintained its stellar levels, and her team adapted to her schedule, showing that a well-negotiated compromise could lead to a harmonious balance.

Similarly, there's Sophia, a tech entrepreneur who frequently travelled for business. Amid the demanding schedule, Sophia utilised technology to remain virtually present at home, joining family meals via video calls and ensuring her presence was felt despite the physical distance. She also enlisted the support of local family members and a reliable childcare network to provide stability at home.

Another example is Lina, a corporate lawyer with an expansive portfolio of high-stakes cases. She harnessed the power of delegation both at work and at home, relying on junior colleagues to handle routine legal tasks, while she focused on high-level strategy and client relations. At home, Lina shared parental duties with her partner equitably and employed domestic help to manage household chores, allowing for quality family time during weekends.

A poignant narrative comes from Priya, a seasoned executive in a multinational firm, who succumbed to a health scare that prompted a radical change in her life. She restructured her work commitments, delegated more, and set boundaries to ensure she could incorporate regular exercise and mindfulness practices into her day. Her health's improvement was a testament to the power of self-care as an essential component of work-life balance.

Beyond the personal stories, organizational case studies also provide valuable insights. For example, a progressive European tech company introduced a four-day workweek without reducing salaries, finding that employees remained productive and were happier and healthier overall. This bold move proved that systemic changes could create environments where work-life balance is encouraged and respected.

In the public sector, the story of a city's mayor, Helena, resonates profoundly. She initiated community programs that supported working parents, such as after-school initiatives and parental support networks – policies that she herself benefited from. Her success demonstrated how solutions for work-life balance could be scalable and influential within larger communities.

On the international stage, Katrin, a diplomat, managed her transnational responsibilities by creating a robust support system with her spouse, who took a career break to focus on their children's needs. Their partnership enabled Katrin to fulfill her duties with the assurance that her family was thriving.

Within academia, we look to the example of Anita, a university dean who, through meticulous planning, managed her administrative duties, teaching commitments, and research work alongside being a single parent. Her approach to time management set a standard for others, proving that academic leadership and parenthood need not be mutually exclusive arenas.

The publishing industry also offers inspiration through editor-in-chief Emily, who instituted flexible working policies in her firm after experiencing the challenge of managing deadlines and daycare drop-offs. Her story influenced industry-wide conversations about workplace flexibility and helped normalize different work patterns.

In sports management, Kaitlyn's journey shines. She lobbied for on-site childcare at her organization, fostering a culture where parents didn't have to choose between career progression and family. By addressing the needs of working mothers proactively, she underpinned the importance of institutional support for work-life balance.

In the arts, we observe a director of a renowned museum, Vera, who combined her leadership role with raising twins by redefining the expectations of her position. She introduced remote working long before it became mainstream, paving the way for a more inclusive approach to balancing professional and private life in the art world.

Each case study underlines a crucial fact: the solutions to achieving work-life balance are as individual as the women themselves. Moreover, these solutions require boldness in renegotiating terms, establishing boundaries, and advocating for personal and organizational changes that facilitate a more balanced life.

These narratives serve as a blueprint for integrating career aspirations with personal fulfillment. They demonstrate that with the right mindset, structures, and support, work-life balance isn't merely an abstract ideal but a tangible reality that benefits individuals, families, and organizations alike.

As we navigate our professional journeys, let us draw inspiration from the tenacity, innovation, and wisdom of these exemplary leaders. They remind us that our endeavors in the corporate world can be harmonized with our personal lives, leading to success and satisfaction in both spheres. Embracing these examples can ignite a profound transformation that resonates beyond individual achievements, shaping the cultural landscape of workplaces around the world.

Chapter 7:
The Importance of Self-Promotion

In navigating the corporate labyrinth, the ability to adeptly showcase one's accomplishments cannot be underestimated, particularly for women who historically may have shied away from the limelight. To thrive in leadership, one must construct an edifice of visibility, ensuring that competencies and achievements are not merely carbon copies of expectations, but are distinguished monuments seen and acknowledged by all. This chapter unearths the subtle yet potent tactics of self-promotion--an endeavour that needn't steal from the currency of humility. Striking a poised balance, this section empowers women to craft a narrative that resonates with authenticity and commands recognition. Delving into the artistry of visibility, the subsequent pages provide a blueprint for articulating value without tipping the scales into braggadocio, weaving together a compelling case for self-advocacy as an indispensable tool in the arsenal of ascendant women in the corporate sphere.

Mastering the Art of Visibility

As we delve deeper into the journey toward the pinnacle of leadership, inherent challenges can eclipse the strides made by female executives. Amidst these, one key element that often goes unaddressed is visibility. It's not simply being seen; it's about being acknowledged for your contributions, being recognised as a potential leader, and being top of mind when opportunities arise.

Understanding visibility entails a multifaceted approach. It's an art that requires astuteness, the kind of self-awareness that aligns one's personal brand with one's leadership aspirations. Visibility is a strategic tool that, when wielded effectively, can lead to impactful opportunities and the dismantling of barriers that inhibit the progression of women to leadership roles.

The question of visibility is not solely about stepping into the limelight. It's about authentic display of one's competencies and value-addition. For many women, this begins with self-promotion, a nuanced skill that strikes the balance between confidently articulating one's achievements and radiating a sense of team-orientated progression.

Self-promotion should be viewed not as bragging, but as an essential component of career strategy. It's about communicating your results and potential in ways that resonate with key stakeholders. This requires understanding the metrics and language that reflect success within your organisation; aligning your narrative with these allows your contributions to be recognised and valued.

Visibility also means contributing beyond your immediate responsibilities. It's about engaging in cross-departmental projects, participating in innovation hubs, or leading corporate social responsibility initiatives. Such contributions demonstrate an ability to operate at a strategic level and showcase leadership acumen beyond one's expected duties.

Engaging with internal platforms, such as joining or initiating a committee or a task force, can also amplify your visibility. These platforms often allow for interaction with senior leadership, offering a stage to showcase not just expertise but leadership potential in a universally beneficial context.

Networking is, undeniably, an integral part of the visibility toolkit. It cultivates relationships that can act as catalysts for recognition. Networking shouldn't be relegated to occasional events but must be embedded into one's professional routine. Establishing a robust, diverse, and strategic network becomes a source of opportunities, insights, and personal brand amplification.

Let's also address the digital domain, where professional platforms like LinkedIn have transformed the visibility landscape. A deliberate online presence, thought-leadership through articles, or participation in relevant forums can extend your influence and visibility beyond the confines of your company.

Thought leadership is another powerful vehicle for boosting visibility. Sharing your insights through speaking engagements, panel discussions, or industry publications positions you as an expert in your field. It commands respect and invokes the recognition of peers and leaders within and beyond your organisation.

Visibility often demands resilience. Women may encounter instances where their efforts go unnoticed or are undervalued. It's imperative to persevere, to seek feedback, to refine one's tactics, and sometimes, to diplomatically advocate for the credit one deserves.

Leading by example and mentoring others is a transformative visibility strategy. By lifting others, you illuminate your capacity not just as a manager but as a leader who paves the way for growth. Your mentorship will reflect your values and multiply your influence as your mentees become ambassadors for your leadership style.

Visibility is not a solo endeavour; it's about harnessing the collective efficacy of diverse allies. Allies can propel your visibility through sponsorship and by advocating for your capabilities in those decision-making spaces where you may not yet have a seat.

Patience is integral to mastery, as the art of visibility doesn't yield immediate results. It's a career-long pursuit that evolves with the landscape of your professional milieu. One must be strategic in choosing when to shine and when to empower others to do so.

And so, as one navigates the corporate world, remember that mastering the art of visibility is not just about elevation in the present. It is an investment in one's legacy as a leader and a contribution to reshaping the corporate world to acknowledge and celebrate the indispensable role of women in leadership.

Cultivating visibility as a female leader holds the potential to not only advance your personal career but also to lay the groundwork for a more equitable professional environment for your successors. In mastering this art, we do more than succeed - we redefine the essence of leadership for generations to come.

Balancing Confidence with Humility

In the paramount journey towards empowering women in corporate leadership, a delicate equilibrium must be achieved—a balance between projecting confidence and demonstrating humility. Often, society expects women to straddle the line between assertive and nurturing, authoritative and accommodating. This dichotomy, while challenging, can be navigated with grace and intention.

Confidence is the currency in the realm of leadership; it's an indication that one possesses the knowledge, competence, and capability to lead. It propels women to be seen and heard in environments where their presence is often undervalued. However, overconfidence can lead to missteps or the misperception of arrogance—traits often unfairly ascribed to women who assert themselves. It's essential then, to cultivate a self-assuredness that is perceived not as overbearing, but as assertive and decisive.

Equally important is humility—a trait that has the strength of its own. It enables leaders to acknowledge their limitations, learn from others, and continuously evolve. Humility in leadership fosters an inclusive environment, opening doors for collaboration, and the synthesis of diverse ideas. Importantly, it allows leaders to form genuine connections with their teams, building trust and loyalty.

To strike the right chord between confidence and humility, it's vital to embrace self-awareness. This involves regular introspection, acknowledging one's achievements without boasting and recognising areas for improvement without self-deprecation. Self-awareness is the compass that guides leaders in how they carry themselves, inject their viewpoints, and manage their interactions.

A manifestation of this balance is found in the ability to advocate for oneself while celebrating others. Women in leadership must not shy away from showcasing their accomplishments—owning success is pivotal for career advancement. Yet, they must also acknowledge the collective efforts of their team, sharing credit where it's due. This shows both confidence in one's own abilities and humility in recognising the power of the collective.

In communicating one's vision and goals, clarity and persuasive conviction must be underpinned with openness to feedback and alternative perspectives. This approach demonstrates the leader's belief in her strategies, coupled with the wisdom to pivot based on insightful input.

Indeed, learning to receive and dispense feedback effectively is an art in itself. It requires a leader to balance strength with vulnerability. By actively soliciting feedback, a leader highlights confidence in their ability to grow. And by giving constructive feedback with empathy, they display a humility that uplifts and empowers their team.

Yet, the drive to achieve this balance should not be mistaken for a push towards perfection—a pitfall laden with unrealistic expectations. Leaders are human, and it's their humanity that often inspires others to follow them. Acknowledging mistakes, therefore, should not be a source of shame but a badge of honour, signalling both courage and humility.

Another dimension of this balance lies in negotiation scenarios. An effective negotiator stands her ground, confident in the value she brings to the table. At the same time, she remains amenable to compromise, understanding that flexibility can yield mutually beneficial results. She's guided by a vision of success that is inclusive of shared gains.

Networking, too, is an arena where the balance is crucial. Within these professional ecosystems, the ability to assert one's experience and pull one's weight is as necessary as listening and offering support to others. A well-nurtured network is built on the foundation of reciprocal relationships, where confidence in one's ability to contribute is met with a humility to learn from the experiences of others.

As women ascend the leadership ladder, they'll often be scrutinised more harshly than their male counterparts. It's in these moments that balancing confidence with humility becomes an act of defiance against gender norms and stereotypes. It's a poignant stance that commands respect while fostering an atmosphere of gender equality.

Moreover, women leaders should apply this balance in mentoring others. By confidently guiding their mentees while humbly learning from them, they cultivate a new generation of balanced leaders. This two-way street of knowledge and experience enriches the mentor as much as the mentee.

In this spirit, women in leadership roles must not only exercise this balance themselves but advocate for a culture that values it. By promoting environments that appreciate both confidence and humility, they pave the way for more inclusive, collaborative, and effective leadership.

Ultimately, the symphony of confidence and humility tunes into the heartbeat of effective leadership. When skilfully rendered, it resonates with authenticity—inspiring trust, commanding respect, and dismantling barriers.

Therefore, as women continue to rise and reshape the corporate landscape, this duality must be harnessed. It's not about diminishing one's light but rather about shining in a way that illuminates paths for others. It's about being bold in vision and gentle in approach, strong in resolve and open in perspective—a true testament to the dynamic capabilities of women in leadership.

Chapter 8:
The Support System: Family, Friends, and Foes

In the intricate tapestry of a leader's journey, the threads of family, friends, and foes interweave to create a complex support system that can bolster or challenge a woman's rise to the top. Family may serve as a cornerstone, providing emotional anchorage and practical assistance, yet it's equally vital to recognise when familial expectations could tether one's ambitions. Friends, those who cheer from the sidelines and offer unyielding encouragement, are instrumental in bolstering one's resolve during turbulent times. However, it's essential to remain cognisant of the indelible impact foes can have, those whose resistance strengthens our resilience and forces us to refine our strategies. Acknowledging the roles each play, we can weave a network that sustains us, a buffer against the barrage of challenges faced in corporate ascendancy. Through embracing the support and learning from opposition, women can carve out leadership paths defined by tenacity, adaptability, and unwavering determination.

The Role of Family

Is an undeniably significant factor in the journey of any professional, and for women aiming for leadership roles, it often takes on a multifaceted dimension. The family environment from which one hails and the family one nurtures can both carve and divert paths in the landscape of corporate leadership. This sphere of personal life has the potential to be both a grounding force and a challenging frontier for the aspiring female leader.

Historically, the role of women has been perceived primarily through the lens of familial responsibilities. In many cultures, women were – and sometimes still are – expected to prioritise the home over professional aspirations. Yet, as we witness transformational shifts in societal norms, the conversation around the role family plays in fostering or hindering women's leadership ambitions has broadened.

For women in leadership, the support of family can serve as a cornerstone, providing emotional sustenance and practical assistance. When family members are allies in one's aspirations, they can contribute significantly to balancing the varied demands that come with climbing the corporate ladder. This support system can take many forms, from a partner sharing domestic responsibilities, to extended family stepping in during demanding professional periods, to the moral support that can buoy a leader during challenging times.

Nevertheless, one cannot overlook the complexities that arise when navigating family expectations alongside professional growth. Female leaders frequently find themselves straddling the fine line between meeting workplace expectations and fulfilling familial roles. Challenging as it may be, it demands a renegotiation of traditional roles and responsibilities within families to ensure that their support dovetails with professional commitments rather than contradict them.

Families also play a critical role in sculpting early leadership traits. The encouragement of independence, critical thinking, and fostering a sense of confidence during formative years lays the foundation for leadership potential to flourish. Conversely, the absence of such support can significantly curtail ambition and self-belief, with long-term implications on career trajectories.

For women with children, the family dynamic introduces additional nuances to the leadership journey. Motherhood and executive leadership are both intensely demanding, and mastering the synchronisation of these roles requires tenacity and resilience. It often necessitates a system of flexible work arrangements, equitable partnership at home, and if fortunate, accessible childcare support.

This intersection between parenthood and professional ambition brings to light questions around maternity leave and its impact on career progression. Despite strides made in policy and perception, the perceived penalty of taking maternity leave persists, influencing career choices and sometimes deterring women from pursuing leadership positions. Familial support in this context doesn't simply mean providing care during the leave period, but also bolstering the leader's decision and advocating for her professional value upon return to the workforce.

Familial influence extends beyond immediate relatives; the larger family network can be instrumental in facilitating opportunities through connections, acting as sounding boards for ideas, or providing advice based on their own experiences. This rich tapestry of interactions shapes a woman's leadership ethos and her approach to navigating the corporate world.

It is, however, critical to acknowledge that not all family structures are supportive. Some may actively dissuade or obstruct a woman's ambition. Female leaders often find themselves carving their path in spite of familial resistance, which requires an exceptional level of determination and a strong belief in one's own leadership vision.

In situations where the family paradigm does not align with career ambitions, seeking a chosen family can be incredibly powerful. This alternative support system – built on the foundations of mutual respect, understanding, and shared aspirations – can provide the emotional and operational support needed to climb the corporate peak.

An important consideration for women leaders is the reciprocation of support. As they receive backing from their family, it is equally vital for them to invest in their family's growth and well-being, nurturing an environment of mutual support. Success is not one-dimensional, and it is enriched when shared and supported by loved ones.

Aspiring female leaders must, therefore, be adept at managing family dynamics and setting boundaries that are respectful yet firm. Communication is key in delineating professional ambitions and advocating for the space to pursue them. The art of negotiation, often discussed in the corporate realm, finds a deeply personal application in the context of family.

The narrative that a woman must choose between family and leadership is an outdated one. As modern corporate structures evolve to embrace more inclusive family policies, the hope is for a future where women in leadership do not find themselves isolated in their pursuit but celebrated and supported by their families.

The lexicon of leadership is dotted with attributes that are often nurtured within the family setting. Traits such as resilience, emotional intelligence, and integrity are at times a reflection of one's family influence. It underscores the idea that while the individual may blaze the trail, the family often lays the stones that pave the path.

In conclusion, the role of family in a woman's climb to corporate leadership is both a bastion of strength and a potential source of struggle. It's a confluence of the past's shaping forces and a partnership for the future. As female leaders, one's task is not to diminish the importance of family but to innovate ways through which it can serve both the heart and the ascent to professional zenith.

Dealing with Resistance

The path to leadership for women is often fraught with resistance. Be it subtle unease or overt pushback, resistance can stem from various quarters—peers, subordinates, or even from those within one's support system. Yet, acknowledging this resistance is not an admission of defeat; rather it's the first step towards formulating a robust approach to tackle it. How does one then address and dismantle such resistance? Let us delve into strategies that not only challenge the status quo but also empower the individual and her allies.

Understanding the root of resistance is critical. Sometimes, resistance is a byproduct of fear—fear of change, fear of the unknown, or fear of loss of status or comfort. In the corporate maze, a female leader might find herself in situations where her authority is questioned or undervalued. Remember, cracking the code of resistance requires patience and a strategic mindset. It's important to approach each instance of resistance as an opportunity for dialogue and education, rather than confrontation.

Communication is your sword and shield in these scenarios. It is one's prowess in articulating vision and aligning it with the broader goals of the organization that often quells the fires of resistance. Persuasive communication should not be confused with aggression; it's the art of winning over your audience with logic, emotional intelligence, and an inclusive language that envelopes even the most sceptical critic.

Never underestimate the power of role modelling. As a female leader facing resistance, how you handle it can set an example for others. Displaying confidence and resolve in the face of adversity can inspire other women in the organization, signalling that such challenges can be overcome with grace and determination. This bolsters the collective resilience of the entire team or organization.

An effective leader doesn't just lead; she listens. Even when dealing with resistance, it's important to maintain open lines of communication. This means actively seeking out feedback and demonstrating a willingness to consider different perspectives. Resistance often dissipates when people feel heard and understood, and their concerns are addressed earnestly.

Engage in coalition building. You can't do it alone and you shouldn't have to. Identifying allies within your organization helps you to create a support network. These individuals can include colleagues at the same level, supportive superiors, and mentees who feel invested in your journey. Their collective endorsement and support can act as a counterbalance to the detractors, and their insights can be invaluable.

Consistency in your leadership style also plays a pivotal role. It's the bedrock upon which trust is built. People are more likely to rally behind a leader whose actions and decisions are predictable and aligned with her stated values and goals. Inconsistent behaviour, on the other hand, gives rise to uncertainty and fuels resistance.

Make sure to harness your emotional intelligence. A leader who is adept at reading the room can adapt her approach to suit the audience and mitigate resistance before it festers. Emotional intelligence involves recognizing not just what is being said, but also the emotions and motivations behind the resistance. When you can appeal to the underlying concerns of your opponents, you are more likely to find common ground.

Facing resistance can be a lonely battle, but self-care ensures you don't burn out in the process. It's essential to maintain a work-life balance, remain connected with your passions, and nurture your mental and physical wellbeing. A leader who is burned out will find it much harder to deal with resistance effectively.

Nurture your network outside of your immediate organization. Industry groups, professional networks, and peer circles can provide valuable perspective and support. Such networks can also serve as a source of motivation and resilience when you face internal resistance at your workplace. Learning from others who have faced similar challenges can arm you with new strategies and reinforcements.

Considering resistance as a learning opportunity is an optimistic stance that can facilitate growth. Each instance of resistance gives you insights into the dynamics of your corporate environment and reveals areas that may require additional focus for advancing gender equality. Continuous learning and adapting is a hallmark of great leaders.

Documenting your experiences with resistance can serve multiple purposes. It allows you to reflect on what strategies worked and what didn't, providing a personal case study to refer to in the future. Additionally, this documentation can contribute insights to the broader discourse on women's leadership, offering valuable lessons to others.

While facing resistance, it's essential to keep your ultimate goal in view. Rather than getting bogged down by day-to-day opposition, maintain focus on where you aim to lead your team and organization. Leaders are visionaries; they plot the course through choppy waters with their eyes fixed on the horizon.

From time to time, reassess your approach towards dealing with resistance. What works today may not work tomorrow, and flexibility in strategy is key to outmanoeuvring opposition. As societies evolve, so do organizational cultures and attitudes towards female leadership. Stay tuned to these changes and adapt accordingly.

Finally, celebrate your victories, big or small. Overcoming resistance, changing minds, and making incremental progress deserves recognition. These triumphs galvanise you and your supporters to keep pushing the boundaries. Your successes act as beacons, guiding future female leaders as they navigate their paths.

Resistance can either be a stumbling block or a stepping stone; the outcome is largely determined by your response to it. As a female leader, your journey is not just about reaching personal pinnacles of success but also about paving smoother paths for the women who follow. By confronting resistance with tact, empathy, and unwavering resolve, you are rewriting the narrative—one that speaks of strength, perseverance, and undoubted leadership.

Chapter 9:
Strategies for Effective Communication

As we traverse the evolving landscapes of corporate leadership, it becomes increasingly clear that communication is the linchpin that holds together the mosaic of success. Effective communication is not just about expressing oneself; it's about being heard and understood, fostering environments where dialogue catalyses innovation and collaboration. In this chapter, we delve into how assertiveness can be harmonised with empathy and clarity to resist the undertow of misunderstanding that often bogs down workplace dynamics. It's about equipping women leaders with the linguistic and behavioural toolkits to assert authority without alienating, to negotiate with a balance of firmness and flexibility, and to articulate their vision with an unwavering voice that commands attention and respect. We will explore how nuances in tone, body language, and context can transform conversations into meaningful exchanges that propel careers forward, shape vibrant cultures, and dismantle barriers - enriching the tapestry of interaction with threads of mutual respect and recognition.

Assertiveness in the Workplace

As we delve into the intricacies of effective communication within the corporate sphere, a powerful tool emerges for women in leadership: assertiveness. Historically, societal constructs have often labeled assertive women negatively, associating the quality with unflattering characteristics. However, in the realm of business, assertiveness is a critical component of effective leadership and negotiation. Its judicious application can help dismantle barriers, properly articulate one's vision and goals, and foster a culture of respect and equality. Assertiveness isn't about aggression; it's about clear, confident, and respectful communication.

Assertiveness involves the ability to express thoughts and feelings openly while maintaining respect for others. It strikes a balance between passivity and aggression. Women in the workplace can utilise assertiveness to convey their needs and boundaries without encroaching on others' rights. This approach begins with self-awareness, understanding your values, and recognising the importance of advocating for yourself in a professional context.

Expressing oneself assertively can also mitigate misunderstandings and reduce conflict. Women leaders can set the tone for their teams by modelling assertive communication. It enables them to establish clear expectations, delegate responsibilities effectively, and navigate negotiations with confidence. When a woman communicates assertively, she sends a message that her ideas and contributions are valuable, which often encourages the same behaviour among her colleagues.

There is a delicate line between assertiveness and perceived aggression, one that women often need to tread carefully due to ingrained biases. To do so, women can employ strategies such as "I" statements which focus on their experience rather than making accusatory comments. For instance, "I feel overlooked when my input isn't considered in meetings," as opposed to "You always ignore my suggestions." This not only maintains a collegial atmosphere but also prioritises the speaker's agency and perspective.

Listening is an integral part of assertiveness. It involves paying close attention to colleagues' responses and seeking to understand their point of view. By listening actively, women leaders can identify common grounds and shared objectives, which serve as platforms for collaborative solutions and innovation. Listening transforms the act of assertiveness into a two-way exchange—essential for maintaining collaborative and productive relationships.

Assertiveness also involves setting and enforcing boundaries, which safeguards professional respect and personal wellbeing. Learning to say no—an assertive decline—is as important as making assertive requests. Women leaders especially can highlight the importance of boundaries and lead by example, enabling a work environment where team members feel their limits are understood and respected.

Feedback—giving and receiving—is a cornerstone in the assertive leader's toolkit. Through constructive criticism delivered assertively, women can propel their team's growth and performance. Similarly, welcoming feedback with an open mind exemplifies a commitment to continuous improvement, a quality admired in leaders across all levels.

In the ambitious climb of the corporate ladder, assertiveness aids in mastering the art of negotiation. Knowing one's worth and negotiating for appropriate compensation is vital. Women can harness assertive negotiation strategies to challenge the gender pay gap and advocate for equitable treatment.

Culturally, assertiveness in women has not been uniformly welcomed, unfortunately leading to less utilization of this skill. Women often face a double bind where if they do not speak up, they are overlooked, but if they do, they risk being criticised. Addressing this challenge entails both personal and systematic changes. Organisations need to foster environments where assertiveness is valued and rewarded irrespective of gender. Women can lead this change by embodying assertive traits and breaking down preconceived notions.

Another facet of assertiveness lies in conflict resolution. Assertive communication equips women with the means to navigate conflicts constructively, focusing on problem-solving and achieving resolution rather than resorting to counterproductive avoidance or confrontational tactics.

In addition, assertiveness encourages transparency within the workplace. By openly discussing expectations, concerns, and aspirations, women leaders can engender trust, which is fundamental to building and maintaining strong, functioning teams.

Fostering assertiveness is not a solitary journey; it involves mentoring and peer support. Women can benefit from guidance on how to assert themselves effectively, considering the unique challenges they may face. A supportive network can provide encouragement and strategic advice to refine their assertive communication skills.

It's important to appreciate that assertiveness requires practice. Becoming comfortable with assertive communication often involves stepping out of one's comfort zone. Simulations, role-playing, and real-time practice in safe environments can help women prepare for high-stakes scenarios where assertiveness is critical.

Finally, assertiveness aligns closely with the idea of presence. When women leaders speak and act assertively, they cultivate a commanding presence that can influence the dynamics of a meeting, a negotiation, or an organisation as a whole, shaping outcomes and propelling careers.

Conclusively, assertiveness in the workplace is a skill that can—and should—be honed. It paves the way for effective leadership, allowing women to articulate their vision, lead their teams with assurance, and advance the broader agenda of gender equality. Encouraging a culture where assertiveness is practised and valued is a step toward a more equitable, dynamic, and successful professional world for all.

Negotiation Skills for Women Leaders

As we delve into the art of negotiation for women leaders, it's essential to recognise the unique position women often find themselves in at the bargaining table. Traditionally, women have been stereotyped as less assertive and more cooperative than men. This stereotyping can unfortunately lead to preconceived notions that women are less effective negotiators. However, harnessing one's negotiation prowess is not about gender but mastering a set of refined skills and strategies.

For a start, self-awareness is a cornerstone of successful negotiation. Women leaders can benefit from understanding their negotiation style and how it might be perceived. Are you naturally more accommodating, or do you tend to assert your position? Being able to recognise your style allows for adaptations to be made depending on the context of the negotiation, leading to a more favourable outcome.

Embracing emotional intelligence is also pivotal in negotiations. Women leaders often have high emotional intelligence, which can be a potent asset. By reading the room, empathising with the other party, and managing your emotions during high-stress discussions, you can create a rapport that paves the way to agreement.

Preparation is also critical. Entering a negotiation without thorough research and a clear understanding of both your bottom line and your counterpart's is akin to setting sail without a compass. Women leaders should gather intelligence, define their goals clearly, and understand the needs and constraints of the other party to negotiate from a position of strength.

Setting clear goals and establishing your BATNA (Best Alternative to a Negotiated Agreement) before negotiations commence sets a framework within which you can manoeuvre. It also provides a safety net that ensures you don't agree to terms that are worse than your alternative options. Goal setting doesn't just apply to the negotiation at hand, but also to the development of your skills as a negotiator over time.

In understanding and liaising with the other party, it's vital to listen actively. Listening confers respect and allows you to gather information that could be crucial in steering the negotiation towards a mutually beneficial outcome. It is often more about what isn't said than what is, and tuning into subtext can provide important clues about the other party's priorities and pressures.

Leveraging a collaborative approach can shift the dynamics from adversarial to cooperative. Women can excel in this by framing negotiations around problem-solving rather than competition. This creates an environment where both parties are working together towards a solution, often leading to more creative and satisfactory outcomes for all involved.

To address the gender dynamics in play, it's important for women leaders to be mindful of how they communicate assertiveness. It's a delicate balance to be assertive without being labeled as aggressive – an unfair double standard that is often applied to women but far less to men in leadership. Exercises in language and tone can be instrumental in managing this aspect of negotiation.

Increasing your negotiation efficacy doesn't happen overnight but through reflection and practice. After each negotiation, women leaders ought to conduct post-mortems to assess what worked, what didn't, and why. This cultivates an ongoing learning process that hones negotiation skills progressively.

Empathy should be wielded as a strategic tool. The ability to understand and share the feelings of another can provide valuable insights into the needs and motivations of those across the table. By understanding their perspective, you can address their concerns and motivations, potentially finding a pathway to consensus that may not have been apparent at the outset.

Women leaders shouldn't shy away from leveraging their networks in preparation for and during negotiations. Seeking advice, perspectives, and even role-playing scenarios with trusted colleagues or mentors can provide a distinct advantage. There's strength in numbers, and elevating your negotiation skills can be a collective effort.

Sometimes, negotiations will involve high stakes or complex issues that might require a third-party intervention. In such cases, women leaders should be open to engaging mediators or facilitators to guide the process. It's a sign of strength to know when to call upon expert advice and support.

Throughout the negotiation process, maintaining integrity and consistency is key. By being dependable and principled, women leaders can build a reputation that engenders trust and respect. In the long term, this can open doors to more successful negotiations and professional relationships.

When an impasse is reached, having the courage to walk away is as important as sealing the deal. Women leaders must understand that not every negotiation will end successfully, and that's perfectly acceptable. Recognising when a situation is irreconcilable allows you to conserve energy and resources for opportunities where agreement is possible.

To break through barriers, women leaders sometimes need to negotiate not just for salaries or contracts but for their roles and responsibilities. Expanding your position or challenging the status quo requires a well-calculated approach that is both strategic and persuasive. It's all about aligning your aspirations with the needs and goals of the organisation.

In the quest for equity and par excellence in leadership, honing negotiation skills is indispensable for women. It enhances not only the ability to influence outcomes and make impactful decisions but also contributes substantially to personal empowerment and career advancement. The negotiation table is not just a place of discussion, but a battleground where female leaders can assert their worth and strategically reshape the dynamics of power in business.

Chapter 10:
Decision Making and Risk Taking

In the labyrinth of leadership, the ability to make decisive choices and take calculated risks is paramount—this journey is particularly nuanced for women in the corporate sphere. Within this chapter, we delve into the complex tapestry of decision-making processes that adorn the backdrop of female leadership. We acknowledge the tightrope of risk taken with one eye cast on innovation and the other on perceptive caution. Here, we elucidate the distinctive attributes women bring to decision making, often harmonising intuition with analytical scrutiny, embracing collaboration, and tethering emotional intelligence to strategic thinking. Through a rich compendium of case studies, we shine a spotlight on those audacious moves that redefined industries, propelled careers, and shattered ceilings. They serve as inspirations, exemplifying how, when women step into their power to make impactful decisions and embrace the risks that accompany leadership, they catalyse profound transformations not only within themselves but across the corporate landscape at large.

The Female Approach

In decision making and risk-taking is one that resonates with presence, intuition, and inclusive visioning. This approach represents a blend of strategic acumen with an empathetic understanding of the wider implications of leadership decisions. Women, by nurturing this distinctive approach, have an opportunity to reshape the corporate landscape, offering a compassionate yet powerful edge to modern leadership.

Historically, risk-taking has been painted as a male-dominated arena, depicting a bias that has marginalised female leaders. However, today's female executives are redefining this misconception by demonstrating judicious and effective risk assessment and decision-making abilities that take into account not only the potential gains but also the social and ethical considerations.

The essence of the female approach to decision-making often lies in its collaborative nature. Women leaders are inclined to engage their teams, gather diverse opinions, and reach a consensus that empowers individuals within the organisation. This consensus-building strategy may lead to more sustainable and considered outcomes that account for the complexities of modern business.

Notably, the idea of intuition in business is being revisited through a refreshed lens. Women, who are often lauded for their strong intuition, are leveraging this innate skill to sense market trends and anticipate changes before they become apparent. This preemptive insight is invaluable in navigating the rapidly changing corporate waters and staying ahead of competitors.

Women also face the challenge of unconscious bias and stereotypes that may undermine their authority in high-stakes situations. The female approach encompasses tactics to neutralise these biases by displaying confidence and competence that command respect without compromising femininity. The result can be a richer decision-making process that capitalises on the unique strengths women bring to the table.

Emotional intelligence is another cornerstone of the female approach. Women leaders often exhibit high emotional intelligence, which enables them to read the room, manage conflicts, and maintain team morale even in the face of adversity. They understand that how decisions are communicated is just as important as the decisions themselves.

Moreover, the role of mentorship in molding the female approach cannot be overstressed. Seasoned women executives have the ability to pass on their insights, fostering a supportive environment in which emerging female leaders can take calculated risks with the guidance of experienced mentors.

Ethical leadership is intricately woven into the fabric of the female approach. Women tend to weigh the ethical implications of their decisions heavily, reflecting a broader sense of corporate responsibility. This helps to ensure that the impact of business decisions transcends profit margins and positively affects communities and the environment.

In terms of negotiation, women often combine assertiveness with diplomacy, allowing them to advocate fiercely for their positions while maintaining positive relationships. This skill set is vital when navigating complex deals that require finesse and strategic foresight.

Yet, the challenges remain palpable as women are well aware that missteps can be magnified due to the spotlight on the minority at the leadership table. This awareness can lead to an overly cautious approach, but it also acts as a motivator to thoroughly vet decisions and embrace risk with a calculated and clearly articulated rationale.

The incorporation of flexibility and adaptability into leadership styles comes naturally to many women, given their experiences in multitasking and navigating various life roles. This adaptability allows them to pivot when necessary and embrace innovative solutions with alacrity.

Transparency in leadership is increasingly appreciated in modern corporate culture, and women have been at the forefront of promoting it. Their approach often involves clear communication about the decision-making process, offering insights into the 'why' behind their choices, which fosters trust and creates a loyal following within the organisation.

Inclusive decision-making does not only involve internal stakeholders but also reflects a broader consideration for the impact on customers and society. Women are leading the charge in ensuring that corporate decisions are socially conscious, aligning business objectives with the greater good.

While the stereotype exists that women are risk averse, research and experience are beginning to debunk this myth. Women are indeed taking risks, but they are doing so in a way that is calculated, measured, and informed by a holistic view of potential outcomes. This approach sees women perform a balancing act – one that carefully considers the stakes and the well-being of all parties involved.

In summary, the female approach to decision making and risk-taking is multifaceted and profound, marked by collaborative efforts, intuitive leadership, emotional intelligence, and an unwavering commitment to ethical practices. As women continue to ascend to higher echelons of leadership, this approach has the potential to redefine success not just for women but for the business world at large.

Case Studies on Bold Moves

In navigating the journey of leadership, particularly for women who aim to leave an indelible mark on the corporate map, making bold moves is more than a statement; it's a necessity. Within this intricate tapestry of decision-making and risk-taking, there lies a pool of case studies that offer a luminous beacon—for they are tales of courage, innovation, and strategic gambles that altered the course of businesses and the individuals who led them. Let us explore these narratives, understanding the nuances that powered these bold moves and synthesising their essence to guide and embolden future women leaders.

The first case takes us into the heart of the tech industry, a realm often portrayed as a male bastion. Here, a woman leader proposed a radical pivot from the company's primary revenue-generating product to an untested technology. It was a gamble that could have ended her career, but her insightful market analysis and unwavering conviction swayed the board. She didn't just succeed; she thrived, steering the company to become a market leader in a nascent field. Achieving this required more than just business acumen—she had to muster every ounce of her tenacity and persuasive skills to champion her vision.

Another study dives into the financial sector, where a female executive's decision to overhaul an archaic organisational structure met scepticism. Betting on a flat hierarchy to spur innovation and accountability, she faced stiff resistance. However, by empowering her teams and redefining goals, she facilitated a more agile and collaborative workplace. The firm's subsequent performance outperformed competitors, reflecting how entrenched systems could be reimagined by embracing a bold new paradigm.

Yet another fascinating insight comes from the world of retail, where a leader's bold move to revamp the entire supply chain under the banner of sustainability seemed audacious. While others viewed sustainability as a side initiative, she recognised it as a centrepiece for future-proofing the business. In the wake of her decision, the company not only experienced a surge in brand loyalty but also set new industry standards that competitors scrambled to match.

In consumer goods, a defining moment arose when a woman at the top launched an unprecedented campaign that challenged societal norms. Her company's advertising era had comfortably placed products in idealised settings, but she shifted the focus to real-life stories and the empowerment of women. This move resonated with consumers around the globe, transforming the brand into a symbol of progressive values and advocacy—while also driving sales to record highs.

Manufacturing presents another case where a leader detected an opportunity amidst market saturation. Her decision was to invest heavily in research and development during a downturn, contrary to the prevailing cost-cutting strategy. It was a high-stakes move that questioned her judgement, yet the resulting breakthroughs catapulted the company to lead in innovation, making it clear that sometimes the boldest move is to confront the current and swim upstream.

Healthcare, an industry grappling with constant change, showcases a leader who introduced radical policy changes in response to a burgeoning mental health crisis. Her initiative to integrate mental health support and accessibility into the company's service offerings not only improved care outcomes but also established the organisation as a pioneer in holistic health provision, proving that social consciousness can meld with corporate strategy to yield profound outcomes.

The realm of publishing, faced with the digital onslaught, is where another case unfolds. While watching her competitors slash print runs and downsize, one leader boldly invested in high-quality print editions alongside digital innovations. Her dedication to maintaining the tactile allure of books alongside technological convenience won the hearts—and wallets—of bibliophiles, illustrating that tradition and innovation could indeed reinforce each other.

Meanwhile, in telecommunications, a sector in flux, a decision by a female leader to double down on customer service, rather than cut costs, fostered a customer-centric culture that turned users into brand ambassadors. Customer retention and satisfaction soared, spelling a clear victory for her intuitive understanding of the brand's core value proposition—trust and reliability.

For the renewable energy sector, it was a time for a strategic partnership that wasn't just bold—it was pioneering. When a female leader pushed for an alliance with a tech giant to harness data analytics for energy solutions, many saw it as stepping out of bounds. But this partnership not only led to the optimisation of energy usage but also became the standard for future initiatives, underpinning the profitability of sustainability.

And in the realm of media and entertainment, where storytelling is currency, one leader 's bold move to fund and produce content exclusively by and for women, defied conventional wisdom. The wave of support and the critical acclaim that followed not only solidified the company's reputation for diversity but also filled a niche that had been overlooked by mainstream studios.

Within logistics—a domain seldom recounted for strategic spectacle—a leader's move to automate long before the industry caught on to the trend positioned her company at the vanguard of efficiency. Disruption came with risks and pushback, but her foresight predated the widespread adoption that would follow years later, propelling her company ahead of the curve.

Adventuring into the world of professional services, we find the story of a leader whose bold move was to reimagine not just the service portfolio but the service delivery model. Crafting a mixed virtual and in-person consulting package long before remote work became the norm, she encountered disbelief but received acclaim when the model granted unprecedented flexibility and responsiveness, fuelling growth in a traditionally face-to-face industry.

Lastly, consider the education sector, where a leader capitalised on technological advancements by launching an online learning platform when scepticism about the efficacy of remote education was at its peak. This bold move expanded access to quality education, reinforced the institution's dedication to innovation, and resulted in a smoothly run operation that was primed when the world had to pivot to online learning due to unforeseen circumstances.

What these case studies illuminate is that taking bold moves often necessitates a blend of vision, bravery, and meticulous strategic planning. It requires leaders to anticipate needs, adapt with agility, and articulate their propositions with clarity. For aspiring female leaders, these tales are more than inspirational anecdotes; they are a repository of lessons and strategies that beckon to be learnt from and adapted—a handbook of sorts for crafting one's legacy of bold leadership.

Realising the full strength of audacious leadership moves doesn't come without its challenges—yet, the impact is undeniable. As future female leaders envisage their paths, let these varied, vibrant narratives lend insight and conviction to their aspirations. Harnessing the courage exemplified here will not only shape their own careers but will continue to forge pathways towards an equitable corporate tapestry teeming with diverse leadership at every echelon.

Chapter 11:
Cultivating Executive Presence

In today's corporate arena, cultivating an executive presence is pivotal for women aiming to ascend the ranks. This elusive mix of poise, confidence, and authenticity isn't innate; it's meticulously honed. Gravitas, the weight one carries in a room, is its cornerstone. It's about nurturing a commanding yet approachable demeanour that resonates with colleagues and stakeholders alike. As this chapter unfolds, we'll dissect the components of executive presence and present a blueprint for women to refine their leadership persona. This isn't about transformation into someone you're not; it's about amplifying authentic personal strengths to make an indelible impact. It's breaking through not just the glass ceiling but also permeating the very air of leadership echelons. With focus and determination, it's within reach to not only sit at the table but to also lead the conversation with assurance and influence that are hallmarks of a revered leader. Execution of this calibre isn't just an asset; it's a necessity in the journey to the top.

Defining Executive Presence

As we navigate the landscape of leadership, it becomes apparent that certain intangible qualities often distinguish influential leaders from the rest. Among these is a term frequently discussed yet not always understood: executive presence. But what exactly constitutes this elusive trait? Executive presence is not merely a measure of one's demeanor; it is the embodiment of several interconnected components that project a leader's ability to be taken seriously, inspire confidence, and effect change.

At its core, executive presence involves the way a leader communicates, both verbally and non-verbally. It's in the assurance of their speech, the clarity of their arguments, and the gravitas of their silence. A leader with a strong executive presence can command a room without saying a word—their posture, gestures, and eye contact speak volumes about their confidence and authority.

Yet, executive presence transcends physical communication to include emotional intelligence. Leaders exude executive presence when they show empathy, listen actively, and connect with their followers on a human level. They possess the keen ability to read the emotional current of a room and adjust their approach to motivate and align their team with their vision.

It might seem that executive presence is a quality you either have or you don't, but this isn't the case. It can be cultivated with intention and effort. For aspiring female leaders, understanding the nuances of executive presence is particularly vital in environments that may subconsciously favor male leadership archetypes. Women must navigate these nuances, ensuring they're asserting their presence without being unfairly labeled as overbearing or, conversely, standoffish.

Executive presence is often linked to authenticity. A leader's genuine portrayal of themselves fosters trust and credibility. Women in leadership roles can harness their unique perspectives and experiences to create a presence that is both commanding and relatable. Authenticity in leadership involves no pretense; instead, it requires being true to one's values and principles in all aspects of professional conduct.

Visibility is another key factor in establishing executive presence. Leaders must be seen; their actions, decisions, and contributions recognized. To make an indelible mark, one must be proactive in taking high-profile projects, speaking up during meetings, and seeking platforms where their leadership can be showcased. Visibility increases influence, which is intrinsic to executive presence.

Decision-making ability is a cornerstone of executive presence. Leaders who wield this presence are decisive—they weigh options, consider implications, and make choices with confidence. This doesn't mean they act impulsively; rather, they gather the necessary information and make informed decisions that demonstrate their competence and their ability to steer the ship, even through turbulent waters.

One must consider the importance of adaptability in the construct of executive presence. The capacity to pivot in response to changing situations, to evolve with shifting dynamics, and to exhibit flexibility without losing sight of the end goal is an aspect of executive presence that's often overlooked but is decisive for leadership success.

Furthermore, to define executive presence, we must address the role of resilience. The journey to the top is fraught with challenges and failures. A leader who stands unwavering amidst adversity, learns from setbacks, and bounces back with renewed purpose exudes an unshakeable presence that can galvanize an entire organization.

Yet, executive presence is not without its subtleties. The projection of warmth, for instance, is a delicate balance but one that forms an integral part of a leader's overall presence. It is in the leader's ability to be approachable, to mentor, and to inspire loyalty through a sense of shared purpose and camaraderie that the warmth dimension of presence is forged.

So, how do women cultivate this presence in a corporate world that may have preconceived notions of leadership? It begins with self-awareness—understanding one's strengths, weaknesses, and the impact one has on others. Self-regulation is important; leaders must manage their own emotions and impulses to maintain their executive presence in various scenarios.

At the same time, the cultivation of executive presence involves continuous development. It's a skill honed through experience, seeking feedback, engaging in leadership training, and observing role models who epitomize this trait. It involves a constant process of learning, adjusting, and enhancing one's leadership style.

The articulation of a clear vision is also an essence of executive presence. When a leader outlines an inspiring and strategic vision, it resonates among stakeholders, igniting enthusiasm and fostering a shared sense of direction. The ability to articulate and champion this vision clearly is a powerful element of executive presence.

Lead by example—this age-old adage holds absolutely true when considering executive presence. Actions speak louder than words and setting a standard of excellence in one's own behavior becomes a testament to a leader's credibility and influence, compelling others to follow suit.

In closing, we must recognize that defining executive presence is as much about substance as it is about style. It calls for leaders to be substantive, impactful, and intentional in their approach. As we empower women to step into and flourish in leadership roles, it is crucial to remember that executive presence is not an inherent trait but an increasingly necessary skill that can be developed, honed, and mastered. It is, in many respects, the silent language of leadership.

Developing Gravitas

In the preceding discussions about executive presence, we touched upon the importance of gravitas. As we delve into its development, it is crucial to understand that gravitas transcends mere presentation. It is the very essence of credible leadership. Women in leadership roles often have their authority challenged or undermined, and mastering the ability to convey depth and substance is central to bolstering your credentials and commanding respect.

Gravitas is not an innate trait; rather, it's a cultivated characteristic. One of the fundamental pillars of developing gravitas is confidence. Confidence doesn't shout; instead, it's a quiet assurance. To convey this through your leadership style, start by believing in your expertise and value. Confront self-doubt with evidence of your accomplishments and capability.

Yet confidence alone does not equate to gravitas. Preparation is equally significant. The hallmark of a leader with gravitas is their ability to speak with authority on matters within their remit. This requires thorough knowledge and understanding of the subject matter at hand. Therefore, continuous learning and staying abreast of industry trends is indispensable. With knowledge comes the power to speak with conviction and to contribute effectively to discussions, even in high-pressure situations.

Authoritative communication is a crucial component of gravitas. This means crafting your narratives strategically, ensuring clarity, and being concise. Choose your words wisely; they should demonstrate your understanding and thought leadership. Assertiveness in your communication will also affirm your position — it's vital to express your viewpoints distinctly and with poise, rather than allowing others to overshadow or interrupt you.

Composure under pressure is a quality that distinguishes leaders with gravitas. It's the ability to remain calm and make rational decisions despite the chaos that may ensue. Strengthening your emotional intelligence will aid in navigating high-stress situations, allowing you to respond rather than react. Being perceived as a calming force in the face of turmoil amplifies your gravitas manifold.

Gravitas also involves the art of influence – not through coercion, but through connection and understanding. Mastering this art starts with active listening and empathy. By truly understanding the perspectives and needs of others, you forge deeper connections, earning trust and respect. This empathic leadership is the bedrock of persuasive influence, a key attribute of gravitas.

Consistency in your leadership presence fortifies gravitas. It can't be sporadic; gravitas must be woven into the fabric of your professional demeanour. Others need to know what to expect from you – that you will invariably exhibit integrity, fairness, and reliability. As such, your actions must consistently match your words, epitomizing the authenticity that cements a reputation of gravitas.

Visibility is also instrumental in developing gravitas. You need to be seen leading, contributing, and engaging. However, it's not about drawing attention for attention's sake, but about being present and memorable in crucial moments. Ensure that you make meaningful contributions to conversations and initiatives that align with your leadership vision and values.

Gravitas also has a visual dimension – your personal style and body language. Conveying executive presence through how you present yourself can reinforce the perception of gravitas. Dressing appropriately for your role, carrying yourself with poise, and using gestures that convey assurance all contribute to the gravitas equation. Your physical presence should complement, not detract from, your professional capability.

Feedback is a portal to growth and refinement. Seeking and actually heeding feedback can help to sharpen aspects of your leadership that contribute to gravitas. Encouraging others to provide honest assessments of your leadership style provides invaluable insights that enable you to align your self-perception with how others view you.

To foster gravitas, do not hesitate to tackle the difficult conversations and make the tough decisions when necessary. Exhibiting this kind of courage — even in the face of potential backlash — solidifies your standing as a leader of substance. It's not only about making decisions; it's about owning them, along with their outcomes, regardless of how they unfold.

Moreover, developing gravitas isn't merely about personal advancement. It's essential to extend your gravitas to lifting others. Mentorship and supporting team members displays the kind of leadership depth that transcends individual achievements. Energise and motivate those around you by advocating for their success as fervently as your own.

Reflective practices, such as journaling or meditation, can assist in grounding your leadership and cultivating a deeper level of self-awareness. These practices can help you to internalise your experiences and the lessons gleaned from them, contributing to the richness of your leadership perspective and the gravitas you project.

A part of gravitas is recognising that it doesn't mean having all the answers. Instead, it's about acknowledging what you do not know and having the resourcefulness to seek answers. Such humility, coupled with the drive for knowledge, feeds into a sustainable model of leadership that is both inspiring and grounded in reality.

Ultimately, gravitas is about impact — the ability to inspire, to lead with purpose, and to create a lasting impression that propels positive change. It may be a nuanced and complex attribute to cultivate, yet it stands as one of the most potent facets of female leadership in challenging the status quo and driving towards a more equitable corporate world.

Chapter 12:
Women in Male-Dominated Industries

Despite the progress unveiled in earlier discourses, the journey isn't without its hurdles—nowhere more palpable than in traditionally male-dominated sectors. This chapter shines a light on the formidable challenges that women encounter, and equally, the remarkable triumphs they achieve within industries where their presence is a sweeping defiance against the status quo. We're not simply charting narratives; we're deconstructing the essence of resilience and strategy that characterize women's foray into fields such as construction, mining, and technology. These stories aren't isolated—they signal a pressing call to action for cultural transformation and inclusiveness that echoes across boardrooms and site offices alike. It is within these contrasts that women have forged pathways of leadership, innovation, and excellence, reinforcing the notion that potential is not gendered. Leveraging the power of diversity, women in these industries become not just participants, but influential architects reshaping the business climate with every glass ceiling shattered.

Challenges and Triumphs

Within male-dominated industries, the quest for balance between challenge and triumph is a narrative shared by countless women striving for leadership roles. These industries often present a rugged terrain, where the footprints of women leaders can be rare yet deeply impactful. The barriers may be steep, but the summits reached provide vistas of change and progress.

The challenge begins with piercing through an often thick layer of preconceptions about women's abilities, particularly in fields perceived as requiring a 'masculine touch.' This doubt can be a substantial hurdle, relegating talented women to the periphery of decision-making circles. However, triumph is found in each instance where a woman's insight, capability, and leadership clears the mist of doubt, establishing her rightful place at the helm.

Networking presents its own paradox. While the 'old boys' club' remains pervasive, fortifying barriers to entry, the power of female-driven networks has become a triumph in its own right. These networks are bastions of support, advice, and opportunity, where shared experiences fuel progress for all members. As more women ascend to leadership, these networks strengthen and expand, casting wider nets for the next generation of female leaders.

In the realm of mentorship, the scarcity of female role models in some industries can feel like navigating without a compass. Nevertheless, those who break through serve as beacons, guiding others and demonstrating the attainability of success. Moreover, mentorship has evolved; men who champion gender equity are increasingly critical allies, illustrating that triumph often requires the collaboration and support of all genders.

Work-life balance is an often-cited challenge, laden with gendered expectations and corporate cultures slow to adapt. Yet, as women articulate their needs and design creative solutions, they are reshaping workplace norms. The triumph lies not only in personal harmony but also in institutional change that benefits all employees.

Bias and stereotypes linger like shadows, obscuring women's true potential. Education, frank dialogue, and strong policies are slowly eroding these insidious barriers. Those who stand firm against bias, calling it out and holding their ground, pave the way for a more equitable landscape where triumphs are attributed to merit rather than gender.

Communication in male-dominated environments can be fraught with the challenge of being heard for one's ideas instead of being judged for one's gender. Women are finding their voice, harnessing assertiveness without apology, and redefining power dynamics one conversation at a time.

Decision-making and risk-taking are areas that have traditionally favored men, often because of stereotypical associations with boldness and leadership. Yet, women's triumphs in these domains are increasingly visible, showcasing the multifaceted nature of effective leadership and challenging pre-existing paradigms.

The cultivation of executive presence is another frontier where preconceived notions can hamper a woman's journey. As women leaders define their own authentic style of gravitas, they triumph, countering restrictive molds with diverse expressions of leadership presence that resonate with genuine authority.

Translating personal success into broader industry change can seem Sisyphean, yet it's where individual triumphs gain collective significance. Women in leadership roles often take it upon themselves to instigate diversity and inclusion initiatives, effect policy changes and mentor future leaders, extending success beyond individual gains.

Confronting pay gaps and navigating promotion processes are persistent challenges in male-dominated spheres. However, increased transparency, advocacy for equal pay, and strategic career planning are turning the tide—a victory for equity and a beacon of hope for parity in all aspects of employment.

Entrepreneurship is a battleground where women have made indelible marks, creating innovative businesses and disrupting traditional models. The challenges are monumental, but the triumphs serve as testimony to women's creativity, resilience, and unparalleled drive to succeed.

Board representation and the role of women in corporate governance, though fraught with obstacles of tradition and resistance, is another area where incremental victories accumulate. Each appointment of a woman to a board position reshapes the corporate landscape just a little more towards a balanced vision for future governance.

Finally, coping with failure and setbacks remains an inevitable aspect of striving for leadership positions. Women have had to cultivate a robust resilience, turning these experiences into stepping stones for success. Each recovery is a quiet ode to the strength women possess and a lesson in perseverance for all who aspire to lead.

Within these challenges, we find not only the shadows that define our struggle but also the light of our triumph – the unassailable proof of progress. By celebrating each triumph, however small, we not only recognize the advances made but also inspire a hopeful trajectory for women aspiring to leadership positions within male-dominated industries. This celebration is more than just acknowledgement; it is a call to action for all who wish to play a part in the symphony of change that is reshaping the corporate world.

Industry Spotlights

Within the realm of male-dominated industries, the glimmer of change is becoming increasingly visible. Compelling narratives of women who have carved out leadership roles defying traditional gender norms offer a beacon of inspiration. This section casts a light on several industries, each with its unique challenges and stories of triumphant female leadership.

The technology sector has stood as a pillar of innovation, yet also a monument to evident gender disparities. Women in tech leadership roles are reshaping the blueprint of what it means to lead in a high-speed environment. Their resolve to build inclusive teams and foster creativity offers a sharper competitive edge to businesses. While the numbers still favour male leadership, every female CEO, CTO, or founder who breaks through does not just crack the glass ceiling—they weave a stronger lattice for other women to ascend.

Engineering, often referred to as the bedrock of progress, has had its foundations shaken by the emergence of women who are not just participating but leading. Their technical expertise combined with unique perspectives has led to ground-breaking solutions in civil, mechanical, and aeronautical fields to name but a few. Their participation highlights the importance of diverse thought in solving complex global issues.

The finance industry, an old guard of sorts, has historically been dominated by men. However, women are currently managing substantial funds and making decisions that influence entire economies. By combining astute financial acumen with a nuanced understanding of market dynamics, they're facilitating change not just in gender representation but in fiscal strategy as well.

Moving over to the energy sector, we find that while it is a powerhouse of the global economy, it is also drastically evolving. Female leaders are not only excelling but leading the charge towards sustainable solutions. They're proving critical to the transition to renewable sources, balancing the need for business growth with environmental responsibility.

The construction industry has also seen a seismic shift, with women managing large scale projects and businesses. Their focus on collaboration, risk management, and sustainable practices is not just building infrastructures but rebuilding the industry's ethos from the ground up.

In the realm of defence and aerospace, female leaders are pioneering developments that have strengthened national security and satellite communication networks. They're challenging preconceived notions about women in leadership, demonstrating a capacity for strategic governance and innovation in complex, high-risk environments.

The automobile industry, traditionally a bastion of male leadership, has seen a shift in gears. Women are driving advancements in automotive technology and customer-focused strategies. Their leadership in design, engineering, and marketing is steering the industry into more inclusive and dynamic futures.

Healthcare, a critical industry at the juncture of innovation and empathy, has benefited from a growing number of female executives. Their leadership extends beyond hospital administration to pharmaceutical developments and biotech advancements, where they've become instrumental in guiding responses to global health crises and shaping the future of personalised medicine and patient care.

Within the legal sector, women are increasingly occupying top positions in law firms and judiciary roles. They're bringing a balance to the scales of justice through their keen insight and commitment to fairness and legal integrity. The impact of gender diversity in this sphere extends beyond the courts to influence societal perceptions on rule of law and equality.

Agriculture, an industry as old as civilisation itself, is blooming anew with female thought leaders. They're introducing sustainable practices, championing organic farming, and ensuring food security through innovative agricultural technology. Their nurturing approach has a significant impact on community development and global food policies.

The media and entertainment industry, a cultural influencer, has started to rewrite its script with more women in executive producer and directorial roles. Female leaders are crucial to developing content that reflects a diverse society and challenges gender stereotypes. Their viewpoint is crucial in shaping media that entertain, educate, and inspire.

In the world of sports management, women are propelling significant changes. With leadership roles from team management to head of associations, they are not just influencing how sports are played, managed, and marketed, but also how they can become platforms for advancing gender equality and social justice.

The maritime industry, often overlooked, is witnessing a silent revolution. Women at the helm are navigating through the challenges of a traditionally male domain, managing shipping empires, and pushing for sustainable and ethical maritime trade practices.

Finally, the aviation sector, with its high stakes and complex operations, showcases women leaders who are soaring against the odds. They manage fleets, orchestrate global logistics, and ensure safety in the skies, all while mentoring the next generation of women aviation professionals.

The achievements of women in these industries underscore the broader truth: leadership is not a matter of gender but of capability, vision, and courage. With each success story in these diverse fields, women are not merely filling roles—they're transforming the essence of leadership itself. The ripples created by these industry spotlights set a precedent, encouraging more women to step forward and leave their indelible mark on the corporate world. And as they do, the narrative of what it means to lead will continue to evolve toward a more inclusive, dynamic, and equitable future.

Chapter 13:
Tackling the Pay Gap

In confronting the entrenched issue of the pay gap, it's critical to pierce through the shrouds of reticence and address the stark inequality that lingers in the corporate corridors. It's not enough to acknowledge the pay disparity; active and robust strategies are essential to bridge this economic chasm. Understandably, a thread of frustration might weave itself into the fabric of our discussions on fair compensation, but let us convert that into a galvanising force. The tools for negotiating equal pay are not just swords for battle but instruments of justice, aiming to sculpt a corporate landscape where one's gender does not dictate their financial worth. As we dissect and comprehend the nuances of this disparity, let's arm ourselves with knowledge and negotiate with unwavering tenacity to ensure that women's contributions are valued to the same, unequivocal standard as our male counterparts.

Understanding the Disparity

When we discuss the pay gap between genders in the corporate landscape, we are delving into a complex issue with roots that are deeply embedded in societal, organisational, and psychological grounds. This disparity is not merely a difference in numbers; it signifies an underlying systemic challenge that requires meticulous unpacking. We know the statistics; they are widely reported and often cited in discussions on workplace equality. Nonetheless, the numbers don't tell the whole story. We must scrutinise the underlying causes if we are to address this inequality with any hope of meaningful change.

First, it is essential to recognise that the gender pay gap is often more pronounced the higher up the corporate ladder one looks. This is not a coincidence but a reflection of the myriad invisible barriers that exist for women. While entry-level positions might see men and women start on relatively equal footing, disparities widen as careers progress. The unfortunate reality is that despite having the same qualifications and capabilities as their male counterparts, women are less likely to be offered promotions, high-stakes projects, and opportunities for visible leadership that often lead to higher compensation.

Secondly, negotiations—or a lack thereof—play a significant role. Women are often socialised to be less assertive in salary discussions, which can result in them accepting initial offers without negotiation. Consequently, over time, these missed increments add up to significant financial losses. Moreover, even when women do negotiate, they can face pushback or negative perceptions, unlike men who are expected to, and often rewarded for, assertiveness in these situations.

Another contributing factor is the phenomenon known as occupational segregation. Even today, many industries and roles are heavily gendered, with so-called 'women's work' typically being undervalued and underpaid compared to 'men's work'. This has a profound impact on the overall earnings of women and paints a picture of a workforce where historically constructed norms continue to exert influence over economic realities.

Furthermore, women are disproportionately represented in part-time roles, often due to traditional caregiving responsibilities. This situation penalises them not only in terms of reduced wages but also in terms of pension accruals, benefits, and career progression opportunities. Despite significant societal advances, the burden of balancing work and family life continues to fall more heavily on women, hampering their ability to compete on an equal footing in the workplace.

Maternity leave and the process of returning to work after childbirth also contribute to the pay gap. Many women find it challenging to regain their professional momentum, and in some cases, their absences are viewed unfavourably, affecting their chances of promotions or raises. There's also the 'motherhood penalty' – a documented decrease in earnings for women with children relative to those without – which has no comparable 'fatherhood penalty' for men.

Describing these challenges is not excusing them; it's about laying the groundwork for understanding and, subsequently, transformation. If one doesn't fully comprehend the causes, the solutions will at best be superficial. It's crucial to dismantle the notion that the pay gap is the result of women's individual choices and acknowledge the complex interplay of factors that limit these choices.

Moreover, it's essential to discuss unconscious bias and how it permeates decision-making processes within an organisation. Bias can affect hiring decisions, performance evaluations, and even day-to-day interactions that, cumulatively, can create an environment where women's contributions are undervalued or overlooked. And we know that when contributions are undervalued, so too is compensation.

What is evident is that this isn't just a women's issue; it's a societal one that has implications for family stability, economic growth and corporate performance. A paying workforce is a motivated and loyal workforce, which translates into increased organisational success. Addressing the pay gap, therefore, is not about charity; it's a strategic imperative.

It's often said that what gets measured gets managed. In this context, transparency around pay and promotions becomes paramount. Without data, it's nearly impossible to identify patterns or measure progress. Encouraging a culture of openness about compensation can help identify and address inequalities.

Leadership also has a role to play. Those at the top of the corporate hierarchy have the power to set the tone and drive change. It's not enough to simply acknowledge the disparity; leaders should be effective allies by instituting policies that help level the playing field, such as unbiased recruitment processes, equitable parental leave, and support for work-life integration.

But let's not wait for change to trickle down from those in power. Every individual has the capacity to make a difference—whether through advocating for oneself and others in salary discussions, mentoring and sponsoring fellow women professionals, or pushing for equal representation in decision-making forums.

In closing, understanding the disparity in pay between genders is a necessary first step towards bridging the gap. It's a multifaceted problem, deeply embedded in both structural and cultural dimensions. Women, and men, need to be equipped with the knowledge and tools to advocate for change effectively. Each action, each conversation, and each policy implemented moves us closer to a world where a person's gender does not determine their economic worth.

As we venture further into this exploration, keep in mind that knowledge is a precursor to power. With greater understanding comes an enhanced ability to dismantle the barriers and injustices that have perpetuated the gender pay gap. Let's channel our collective strength, sharpen our wisdom, and be relentless in our pursuit of an equitable corporate landscape where pay is based on merit and ability, not gender.

Tools for Negotiating Equal Pay

Negotiating for equal pay is not just a matter of asserting one's worth; it encompasses a refined toolkit of techniques and approaches designed to level the playing field. In this section, we delve into the practical tools that can be a catalyst for change. Both an art and a science, negotiation demands preparation, knowledge and skill.

First and foremost, it's essential to research and understand your market value. Websites, industry reports, and salary surveys can equip you with data to back your claims. Once you have these numbers, benchmark your current pay against industry standards. Keep in mind that the context varies by experience, role, and geographic location. Armed with this information, you enter negotiations not with personal anecdotes, but with compelling evidence.

While facts and figures are critical, it's equally important to inventory your accomplishments. Create a log of your successes, contributions and any quantifiable impacts you've had within your organization. These details paint a picture that your employer can't ignore—one where your value shines glaringly obvious.

Developing and rehearsing your 'ask' is an integral step. The language you choose can shift the energy of the negotiation from adversarial to collaborative. Instead of demanding what you believe you're owed, frame your request as a question—perhaps, 'How can we work together to ensure my compensation reflects the value I bring to the company?'

Understanding your employer's perspective is also key. They may be bound by budget constraints or other factors. By demonstrating that you grasp the broader picture, you open up the dialogue for creative solutions—maybe it's not just salary, but a combination of benefits, bonuses, and other compensation that could equate to a fair package.

Preparation goes beyond numbers and negotiation techniques. Embrace the reality that emotional intelligence plays a significant role. Understanding non-verbal cues, managing your emotions, and empathizing with the other party are all tools that can win you allies in the negotiation process.

When the moment arrives to negotiate, practice assertiveness—a balance between aggression and passivity. It is not about domination; it is the ability to express confidently and firmly your needs and boundaries without infringing on the rights of others.

Negotiation is an ongoing process, not just a single meeting. It will require follow-ups and potentially several rounds of discussion. Patience and persistence are vital, ensuring that your request remains on the agenda and isn't lost in the daily grind of corporate priorities.

One can't overlook the importance of timing. Aligning your request with performance reviews or the completion of a major project can amplify its effectiveness. In the cyclical nature of business, timing can mean the difference between approval and deferment.

Taking stock of alternative offers can reinforce your position. Although leveraging other job proposals as a threat is not always wise, understanding your options instils confidence and can subtly convey your marketability to your employer. However, use this information with care; your goal is to foster goodwill, not burn bridges.

Mentors can also provide insider knowledge on the negotiation process within your specific industry or company. Don't hesitate to tap into the wisdom of those who have walked the path before you; their guidance on the subtleties of corporate culture can be invaluable.

Role-playing negotiations with a trusted colleague or mentor can iron out any kinks in your delivery. Such practices enable you to field potential questions and objections with grace, ensuring you're not caught off-guard when the stakes are real.

To cement your case, consider this: build allies within the organization who can champion your cause. When others attest to your value, it amplifies your message, making it more persuasive and harder to ignore.

It's vital to document agreements reached in negotiations in writing. This removes ambiguity and records commitments from both parties, providing you with a benchmark for future discussions and ensuring clarity in the commitments undertaken.

Evaluating the outcome with a critical eye is just as important as the negotiation itself. What went well? What could be improved? This reflection sharpens your skills for the future and helps you navigate the ever-evolving landscape of your career with agility and insight.

In essence, negotiating for equal pay is a multifaceted endeavour that blends robust research, strategic timing, emotional intelligence, assertiveness, and the support of your professional network. With these tools at your disposal, you're not only advocating for your personal advancement but also propelling the momentum towards closing the gender pay gap—a noble and necessary pursuit for the corporate world's progression towards full equality.

Chapter 14:
The Role of Women in Corporate Governance

As we delve into the intricate dynamics of corporate governance, it becomes evident that women's involvement is not just a token gesture towards diversity but a fundamental attribute that drives ethical stewardship and innovative perspectives. Women's presence in the boardroom has been statistically linked to enhanced decision-making, robust risk management, and a broader understanding of consumer trends which, in turn, resonate with a more diverse marketplace. It is evident that when women lead, corporate governance evolves—steering away from unilateral, profit-only objectives towards a wider remit that encompasses sustainable practices, corporate social responsibility, and a work ethos that champions inclusivity. The nuanced insight and collaborative spirit that women bring to the table can't be overstated; they often foster a culture of transparency and accountability, which is crucial in today's business climate. Therefore, the role of women in corporate governance doesn't just augment the operational parameters but fundamentally revitalises them, setting a precedent that infuses organisations with resilience and a vision that is equipped to adapt and flourish in the ever-changing business landscape.

Board Representation

Stepping beyond the threshold of acknowledging the disparity in corporate leadership, we now delve into the pivotal role of women on boards. Suffice to say, the tapestry of governance is richer and more effective with strands of diverse perspectives. Tangible change in corporate culture sees its genesis in boardrooms where decisions are shaped and futures delineated.

Women on corporate boards bring a dimension of diversity that nurtures robust decision-making and reflects wider societal diversity. Precisely because these tables of power historically lacked their voices, the inclusion of women is not a mere token but a strategic move; it is akin to unlocking a multitude of potentials that have hitherto remained untapped.

Board representation for women is not merely about achieving a statistical balance, but rather fostering an environment where their insights create ripples of change. Women directors have been associated with enhanced corporate governance and ethical practices, which subsequently can lead to improved financial performance. This reinforces the notion that equity in leadership is not just a social imperative but an economic one.

Challenge is inherent in the quest for inclusion. Possible approaches for increasing representation include proactive recruitment policies, mentoring programmes designed for potential female board members, and continuous education of existing members on the benefits of gender-diverse boards.

However, the path to the boardroom is often laden with implicit biases. Conscious efforts are needed to dismantle the barriers that prevent the consideration of qualified women for these elite roles. This includes addressing the paucity of women in the pipeline leading to executive leadership and consequently to board positions.

Regulatory efforts have proven to be key levers for change in various jurisdictions. For instance, quotas have been instituted in some European countries, mandating a minimum percentage of women on boards. While quotas have sparked contention, their effectiveness in markedly increasing representation cannot be negated. They serve as a pragmatic, albeit abrasive, tool to hasten the pace of gender parity.

Evolving beyond quotas, there exists a burgeoning advocacy for a cultural onus, where organizations self-impose targets for diversity. This shift towards self-regulation represents an advancement in corporate responsibility and a declaration of commitment to gender equality.

One cannot, in this conversation, eclipse the intrinsic value that women bring to the table. They proffer unique perspectives borne out of variegated experiences. They confront groupthink and propel corporations towards previously unforeseen opportunities for growth and accountability.

Visibility matters; seeing women in these high echelons has a multiplier effect. It serves to inspire, galvanise, and forge a path for others. The presence of women on boards is demonstrative in showing female professionals the attainability of such positions, thus perpetuating a cycle of ambition and accomplishment.

Equally important is the preparation of women to take on these roles. There is a profound need for training that equips them with the acumen demanded by governance responsibilities. Professional development workshops, advanced business education, and mentorship are all facets that can secure their board readiness.

A closer inspection of board dynamics also brings to light the necessity for allies within. It's incumbent upon male colleagues to champion the cause of gender diversity. They must harness their influential positions to advocate for, endorse, and sponsor their female counterparts.

Networking skews prominently in the narrative of board representation. Ultimately, boards are congregations of influence, and gaining entry often hinges on connectivity. Women must be given fair access to these networks and encouraged to forge meaningful connections that can catalyse directorship opportunities.

It is crucial to benchmark progress, to measure and publicly report on the strides made in diversifying boards. Transparency lays a foundation of accountability and provides impetus for continued evolution. External pressures conjoined with internal aspirations steward an environment ripe for change.

In the broader discourse, let it be recognised that change is incremental and perseverance is vital. Each appointment of a woman to a board position is not just a personal victory but a collective advance. It punctuates the narrative of corporate progress, engraving in stone the considerable strides towards gender equality.

The purview of governance — once an almost exclusive dominion of men — is being recalibrated. Women are not only entering the fray but also redefining it. The conversation around board representation is a clarion call for more than diversity. It seeks to engender a new dialogue where women are integral to the topography of corporate decision-making, effectuating a legacy of inclusivity and equity for posterity.

Influencing Policy and Culture

As we delve into the arena of corporate governance, it's clear that women have a distinct and pivotal role to play in influencing both policy and culture. The fabric of business isn't just woven with the threads of profit and performance, but also with the patterns set by policies that govern the way organisations behave and the cultures that define what they stand for. Women leaders are not merely participants in this realm; they are curators of change, influencers with the potential to reshape the corporate landscape.

For women who've reached positions of influence, the power to drive policy changes that facilitate gender equality is immense. Modifying policies to ensure equal pay, parental leave, and flexible working conditions can ignite significant transformation. When women in governance roles prioritise these aspects, they lay down the groundwork for a culture that values diversity and advocates for a more inclusive workspace.

Yet influencing culture goes beyond policy amendments; it's about setting a tone that permeates through every level of an organisation. It's the embodiment of values in daily interactions, the steadfast commitment to ethical practices, and the genuine care for employees' well-being. Women leaders can cultivate environments where collaboration trumps competition, where mentorship and support are integral to progression, and where respect is the cornerstone of the professional relationship.

The transition towards equitable corporate governance is burdened with resistance. Women at the helm can expect to face opposition, perhaps even skepticism, but it's through persistent advocacy and embodying the principles they preach that the tide turns. Their unique perspectives and life experiences endow them with a nuanced understanding of the intricacies at play in shaping a fair and forward-thinking culture.

Boardrooms that historically echoed with a single gender's voice are now slowly resounding with a diversity of opinions. Women on boards are not only representing a gender but also bringing distinct insights that can lead companies to more holistic decision-making. This diversity in thought leads to the disruption of unproductive patterns and assumptions, fostering an incubator for innovation.

At the core of influencing policy is the communication of clear objectives backed by data-driven arguments. When proposing policy shifts that favour gender equality, it's essential to present unmistakable business cases that demonstrate the value of these changes. Advocating for gender diversity isn't just about fairness; it's about enhancing business performance. Studies have repeatedly shown that diverse teams lead to better decision-making and ultimately, improved financial results.

A company's culture is often hidden in the nuances of behaviour that's encouraged or dissuaded. As such, women in positions of influence must be vigilant in recognising and addressing subtle biases that can undermine the effectiveness of well-intentioned policies. This might mean championing unconscious bias training, offering support for women's employee resource groups, or spotlighting the achievements of women within the company to serve as powerful role models.

Engaging with stakeholders is another critical component of policy and culture change. Women in leadership must foster relationships with shareholders, customers, employees, and the broader community. By engaging in open dialogues, women can educate stakeholders about the importance of gender inclusivity and enlist their support in advocating for policy changes.

It's not enough to make policy changes; the real measure of success is in their adoption. Implementation strategies must be designed with the full spectrum of employees in mind. Training programs, seminars, and workshops can be effective ways to instill new values and policies into the corporate bloodstream. Such efforts ensure that policy changes aren't just words on a page but are alive in the day-to-day operations of the business.

Measuring the impact of these changes is also vital. By keeping a close eye on the metrics — whether it's the gender ratio in leadership roles, the pay gap, or the retention of women post-maternity leave — leaders can understand the effects of their initiatives. Regular reporting on these metrics, combined with a willingness to course-correct as needed, ensures accountability and continuous progress.

Let's not underestimate the symbolic power that women in high governance wield. When female leaders openly discuss the challenges they've overcome and the strategies they've implemented, they inspire future generations. Through their stories and visible leadership, they signal to younger women that the path to the top, while not without its challenges, is indeed navigable.

Understanding that change is often incremental is key. While sweeping policy reforms are impactful, so are the smaller, yet consistent efforts that lead to shifts in culture. A series of small changes, when gathered over time, can be transformative and lead to a cumulative cultural shift that makes the corporate environment more hospitable to women leaders.

Lastly, exhibiting personal integrity and accountability is possibly the most potent force for influencing culture. Women who lead by example, who align their actions with their values, and who exhibit the change they wish to see instill a sense of trust and credibility. It's by living out these values that they affirm their commitment and influence others to align with their vision for an equitable workspace.

For every policy influenced and culture shifted, there are countless unseen efforts and unspoken challenges that women leaders face. It's their resilience in the face of adversity, their unyielding optimism for a more equitable future, and their unwavering commitment to their values that forge paths for other women to follow. In influencing policy and culture, they are not merely altering the here-and-now, they're laying the groundwork for a legacy that will empower women for generations to come.

In conclusion, the involvement of women in corporate governance channels has profound implications. By leveraging their experiences, strengths, and leadership, women can significantly influence the policies and culture of their organisations. The end goal isn't just to participate in the conversation or have a seat at the table. It's to lead the discourse, shape the framework, and create an enduring environment where equality isn't a goal, but the norm.

Chapter 15:
Entrepreneurship: The Female Vanguard

In the intrepid world of entrepreneurship, women have begun to claim their ground with a fervour that rewrites the narrative of business creation and growth. This chapter charts the exciting ascent of female entrepreneurs who, braving the challenges that have long skewed the entrepreneurial landscape, are shaping robust enterprises and proving that gender is no barrier to pioneering innovations and industry disruptions. We delve into the vivid tapestry of start-up stories that not only inspire but also serve as guiding blueprints for the next generation of female leaders. This ascension signifies a shift, where fostering an entrepreneurial mindset becomes a cornerstone of modern business success. Highlighting the quintessential traits of tenacity, ingenuity, and resilience, "Entrepreneurship: The Female Vanguard" is a celebration and a call to action, signposting a future with women at the forefront of a revolution in commerce and creativity.

Start-Up Stories

The narratives of start-ups founded and helmed by women hold within them not only the chronicles of businesses but also the tales of overcoming deep-seated barriers, the penchant for innovation, and the unwavering belief in one's vision. These stories are remarkably diverse yet unified by a common thread: resilience in the face of adversity and a collective ambition towards unprecedented heights of success. They are not just accounts of enterprises created but are emblematic of a broader movement towards gender equality in the corporate realm.

The genesis of a start-up is often an audacious blend of necessity and creativity. It can emerge from a gap in the market seen and addressed almost exclusively through a woman's lived experience. Take, for instance, a platform connecting parents to vetted caregivers, a response to the perennial struggle of juggling career responsibilities with the need for reliable childcare solutions. It is in these moments of clarity that potential is transformed into tangible enterprises rooted in personal understanding and societal need.

How these ventures navigate initial funding rounds serves as a case study in tenacity. Female entrepreneurs frequently recount the difficulty in securing capital, a reality steeped in biases that a woman's business acumen may be under-estimated. However, these founders often exhibit an admirable degree of assurance and resourcefulness, tapping into networks, crowdfunding, and angel investors who recognise the value in diversity and innovation.

The milestones achieved by women-led start-ups can be instructive. Defying expectations, they often create workplaces that are inclusive and flexible, setting a standard for corporate culture. They demonstrate through practice that profitability and compassionate leadership are not mutually exclusive but are, in fact, beneficial partners in cultivating successful business models that attract talent and foster loyalty among employees and customers alike.

Consider the growth trajectories of these ventures. They do not simply scale for expansion's sake but grow with intentional strategies that consider long-term sustainability and social impact. The journey may include pivots and adaptations that test the founder's vision, yet the most enduring stories vividly illustrate the power of agility in business – a trait frequently essentialised to successful women in leadership roles.

Partnerships and collaborations, too, feature prominently in these start-up journeys. By aligning with other organisations that complement their mission and enhance their capabilities, women entrepreneurs demonstrate the importance of strategic alliances. Even in the face of competition, there is a recognition that collaboration can lead to a greater share of success than going it alone.

The international scope of many women-led start-ups today reveals an understanding that today's businesses must be globally minded. By embracing cross-cultural perspectives and recognising the uniqueness of various markets, these entrepreneurs are crafting enterprises that are as worldwide as they are local in their influence and reach.

Funding rounds, initial public offerings (IPOs), and acquisition talks tend to highlight the business acumen of these leaders, but often unspoken is the support networks these founders have woven into their success tapestry. From family members who double as informal advisors to peers who provide emotional support, the ecosystem around a start-up is vital. It's this community that buoys the entrepreneur through times both fortuitous and challenging.

Technology also plays a central role in the narratives of many women-led start-ups. Whether they're breaking new ground in fintech, health tech, or e-commerce, female founders frequently leverage cutting-edge innovations to deliver user-centric, solution-driven products that disrupt traditional business practices and pave the way for a new kind of enterprise.

Beyond the success metrics and financial models, start-up stories often touch upon the personal transformation of the women at the helm. Guiding a fledgling company from concept to market is a journey littered with lessons in leadership, self-awareness, and personal strength. It is as much about building a brand and a team as it is about developing a fortified sense of self and purpose.

Equally compelling are the narratives of sustainability and ethical governance that have become synonymous with a number of women-led start-ups. In championing corporate responsibility and environmental stewardship, these enterprises are not just generating profit; they're also reinforcing the narrative that businesses have the power to make a positive impact on society.

However, it wouldn't be painting a complete picture without acknowledging the challenges faced. Harsh scrutiny, the pressure to outperform, work-life congruence tensions, and the experience of operating in male-dominated arenas are stark realities. Stories from the front lines of female-founded start-ups are replete with instances of such hurdles met and navigated with a unique blend of precision and grace.

It is within the crucible of challenge that many female leaders find their signature leadership styles. Start-up stories often evolve into leadership manifestos, compelling testaments to the unique qualities women bring to the table. These qualities, ranging from empathy and community orientation to resilience and inclusive decision-making, are not just 'nice-to-haves' but proven drivers of start-up success and longevity.

The triumphs of women-led start-ups do more than contribute to the narrative of successful entrepreneurship; they contribute to the cultural redefinition of leadership itself. These stories illustrate that the attributes traditionally viewed as feminine can be formidable strengths in business, challenging the status quo and reframing what it means to be a leader in today's competitive environment.

Start-up stories, with their myriad challenges, triumphs, and lessons learned, are indispensable chapters in the ongoing narrative of female empowerment and leadership. They are echoes of progress, beacons of potential, and guides for those who endeavour to follow. Each story is an invitation to envision a world where the leadership landscape is no longer defined by gender, but by the calibre of one's vision, the steadfastness of one's determination, and the inclusivity of one's approach to innovation and change.

Fostering an Entrepreneurial Mindset

In this chapter, we embark on an exploration of the entrepreneurial spirit that drives innovation, creates opportunities, and breaks new ground in a diverse range of industries. Cultivating this mindset is not just advantageous for starting a business; it's a transformative approach that can be applied within any role or organisation to foster growth and effectuate change. It's an empowering stance, especially for women who are persistently rewriting the narrative of leadership and success in the business world.

An entrepreneurial mindset is characterised by initiative, adaptability, resilience, and a willingness to embrace risk. For women in leadership, adopting this mindset means seeing beyond the immediate scope of their roles to identify and seize opportunities for growth, efficiency, or new venture creation. It necessitates a resilient attitude in the face of industry challenges, market fluctuations, and the persistent underrepresentation of women in C-suite roles.

Initiative is a cornerstone of entrepreneurship. Women in leadership can cultivate this trait by staying attuned to the needs within their organisations and industries. Don't just wait for opportunities to present themselves; create them. By being proactive, women can make themselves indispensable, showing a capability for foresight that is invaluable in any business setting.

Adaptability is equally crucial. In a corporate world marked by rapid technological advancements and shifting market dynamics, leaders must be able to pivot and adjust their strategies. For women leaders, this might mean continuously skilling up, staying on top of industry trends, and being open to new ways of working. This adaptability also extends to overcoming biases, where rigid gender expectations can often inhibit women's opportunities to lead and innovate.

A resilient mindset is also pivotal. The path of leadership is strewn with obstacles; how one responds to setbacks defines their character as a leader. Women can foster resilience by viewing failures as learning experiences. Embracing a mindset that is not deterred by failure but is encouraged by the growth it brings is vital for anyone looking to make their mark in the business world.

Risk-taking is another integral part of entrepreneurship. However, many women have been socially conditioned to be risk-averse. But leadership requires making decisions that may not always guarantee success. To foster an entrepreneurial mindset, it's essential to cultivate confidence in making calculated risks, whether it's championing a controversial project, expanding into an untested market, or pitching an unconventional idea to stakeholders.

Beyond these personal traits, entrepreneurship involves creativity and innovation. As leaders, women can drive change by encouraging their teams to think outside the box and to question the status quo. A leader who creates a culture where innovation thrives is one who understands the heart of entrepreneurship.

Networking also plays a critical role in nurturing an entrepreneurial spirit. Building robust relationships can provide women with the resources, advice, and connections that are essential for any business venture. A diverse network can also offer different perspectives, which is invaluable when entering new markets or when trying to solve complex problems.

A firm grasp of one's strengths and weaknesses is integral to fostering an entrepreneurial mindset. Women leaders can leverage their strengths to their advantage while seeking support or further training for their areas of improvement. Such introspection and self-awareness can pave the way for strategic personal and professional growth.

Integration of technology is, undeniably, a part of modern entrepreneurship. Being tech-savvy enables leaders to make informed decisions about investing in new technologies or streamlining processes with digital tools. For women, this can also mean breaking into the tech space with innovative products or platforms, thus challenging the gender stereotypes within this industry.

Financial acumen is another aspect that cannot be overlooked when fostering entrepreneurship. Understanding the financial ins and outs of a company is critical to making strategic decisions that will positively impact the bottom line. For women, this might also involve seeking funding for new ventures, where a strong grasp of financial concepts can make the difference in securing investment.

Nurturing an entrepreneurial mindset also means staying committed to lifelong learning. Continuously updating one's knowledge and skills is critical to staying relevant and competitive. Leaders should therefore encourage both their personal and their teams' professional development through workshops, courses, and other educational opportunities.

Lastly, fostering entrepreneurship involves mentorship – both seeking mentors and becoming one. Leaders can learn immensely from the experiences of others who have paved the way before them. Similarly, imparting knowledge and guidance to the next generation is an investment in the future of leadership and entrepreneurship.

Through all these facets, it's crucial to understand the broader impact of fostering an entrepreneurial mindset. It's not just about creating successful businesses; it's about inspiring innovation, credibility, and resilience across the workforce. It's about showing that women have a central role to play in shaping the economic landscape, and that their unique perspectives are an asset to the entrepreneurial world.

In conclusion, fostering an entrepreneurial mindset is not an isolated task but a comprehensive approach to business and leadership. It challenges the notion that entrepreneurship is solely about starting a company, but rather showcases it as a foundational element for any successful leader, particularly for women who are continuously redefining leadership within the corporate domain. By adopting an entrepreneurial attitude, women can imagine and realise a corporate world where creativity, risk-taking, and innovation are not just welcomed but are the driving forces behind continued growth and success.

Chapter 16:
Embracing Diversity and Inclusion

With the wisdom accrued from traversing many tiers of corporate hierarchies, we've come to a broad horizon where the landscape reveals the quintessential role of diversity and inclusion (D&I) in crafting successful organisations. Embracing diversity isn't merely about ticking boxes or meeting quotas; it's about enriching our businesses with a plethora of perspectives that spur innovation and drive growth. Inclusion goes beyond just having diversity present; it's about creating an environment where every voice is heard, and every potential is nurtured. When women in leadership champion these values, they set a powerful example, encouraging others to follow suit and thus weaving a fabric of inclusivity that underpins the organisation's culture. As we set our sights on this chapter's exploration of D&I, we aren't just discussing benefits; we're equipping ourselves with the practical know-how to implement initiatives that resonate through every echelon of our businesses. It's our responsibility as leaders to model this behaviour and catalyse the changes that will sculpt a more equitable and thriving corporate world for all.

Benefits for Business and Society

As we delve into the rich tapestry threaded by the prior chapters, illuminating the multifaceted role of women in corporate leadership, it becomes undeniably apparent that the inclusion of female executives carries profound benefits for both business and society. Truly, the impact of harnessing diverse leadership styles is tremendous, echoing across the very fabric of our economies and communities.

First and foremost, diverse leadership teams have been shown to positively affect the bottom line. Companies that commit to gender diversity at the executive level are not just ticking a box for social credibility; they are investing in a proven strategy for financial success. Research demonstrates that businesses with a healthy balance of men and women in leadership positions often outperform their less diverse counterparts in terms of profitability and value creation.

This enhanced performance can be attributed to the variety of perspectives that women bring to the table. Female leaders often employ a more collaborative and inclusive approach to problem-solving and decision-making. By valuing empathy and emotional intelligence, women can foster a work environment conducive to innovation and creativity, essential ingredients for any business that is striving to remain competitive in a rapidly evolving global market.

Moving beyond profitability, the societal implications of gender-balanced leadership cannot be overstated. With women at the helm, businesses are more likely to pursue policies that lead to sustainable practices, community engagement, and an overall increase in corporate social responsibility. These actions resonate not just within the confines of the business but ripple outward, influencing society for the better.

Furthermore, having female role models in top positions can have a profound effect on the workforce. Young women and girls are inspired by seeing leaders who reflect their own gender identity, which in turn motivates them to pursue their own professional ambitions. By encouraging a new generation of potential leaders, we help ensure a reservoir of diverse talent for future roles.

Equality in leadership also speaks to a more equitable distribution of power and resources, leading to societal gains that range from reduced poverty rates to improved family and community wellbeing. When women are economically empowered, they invest back into their families and local neighborhoods, sparking a virtuous cycle of growth and development.

Moreover, when companies actively work to close the gender gap, they send a powerful message about their values. They demonstrate a commitment to fairness and equal opportunity, which can enhance their reputation and, in turn, attract top talent, loyal customers, and dedicated investors who share similar values.

The psychological effects of workplace equality are equally notable. In environments where women are equally represented, all employees are more likely to feel valued and respected. This can lead to higher job satisfaction and lower turnover rates, thereby reducing the costs associated with recruiting and training new personnel.

In terms of governance, female leadership often embodies a more considerate approach to risk, tending toward decisions that ensure longevity and the welfare of all stakeholders. This is not to say women are risk-averse; rather, they consider a wider range of factors and potential impacts before taking strategic risks, ensuring that actions are thoughtfully calibrated.

Female executives tend to also emphasize mentorship and professional development, creating learning opportunities and cultivating the next generation of leaders. This emphasis on human capital is not just a feel-good measure but a strategic one, ensuring that the organization's future leadership pipeline is robust and skillful.

We must also contemplate how gender-balanced leadership influences business innovation. The inclusion of diverse gender perspectives can lead to products and services that more accurately reflect and serve the needs of a mixed consumer base. This can result in increased market share and the opening up of new market segments.

Additionally, gender diversity on boards and in C-suite positions can lead to improved decision-making processes. With a mix of genders, groupthink is less likely to occur, and cognitive diversity is heightened. This means breaking away from entrenched ways of thinking and opening up to new ideas and insights, which is paramount to thriving in today's complex business landscape.

On a broader scale, as businesses become more representative of the societies in which they operate, there is the potential for cross-pollination of ideas between the corporate sector and public policy. Female leaders often champion initiatives that address pressing societal issues, such as public health, education, and gender rights, thereby influencing broader systemic changes.

In addition to societal betterment, businesses that prioritize gender equality in leadership demonstrate significant strides in meeting global sustainability goals. Such commitments are vital as we collectively approach global challenges with the United Nations' Sustainable Development Goals in mind. Women often champion issues like climate action and ethical labor practices within their organizations, aligning business operations with global imperatives for sustainability.

The compounded benefits of having women in leadership positions are clear and manifold: they stretch from enhancing financial performance to reshaping societal norms and priorities. Therefore, it is incumbent upon not just businesses, but all facets of society to recognize and act upon the intrinsic value of gender equality in leadership roles. In doing so, we pave the way for a future that is rich in innovation, prosperity, and equity for all.

Implementing D&I Initiatives

As we explore the broader canvas of diversity and inclusion (D&I) within companies, it's crucial to shift focus from general discussions to concrete actions. Transformative initiatives are not just feel-good policies; they are strategic approaches to set benchmarks, foster inclusivity, and ensure equitable opportunities for all. D&I initiatives are particularly pressing in the context of gender equality, where dynamic and robust action can significantly alter the professional landscape for female leaders.

D&I initiatives can start with a granular understanding of the organisational culture. It's about determining where blind spots exist and where biases have inadvertently been baked into company processes. In this vein, conducting thorough audits of current practices allows for an informed start. These audits must be conducted with a critical eye, examining everything from recruitment to promotion practices, identifying where women are being shortchanged and implementing robust measures to redress these imbalances.

This leads us to the value of setting clear and measurable D&I goals. Aim to define what success looks like for your organization, and make these goals widely known and integrated into your company's ethos. Whether it's achieving a certain percentage of female leadership or implementing mentorship programs to support women's career growth, setting quantifiable objectives creates accountability and constant momentum towards gender equality.

Key to the success of D&I initiatives is gaining buy-in at all levels. Advocating for gender diversity must start at the top, with leaders unequivocally committed to the cause. However, true inclusivity requires grassroots support. Engage employees at all tiers by creating platforms for discussion and encouraging feedback. When team members feel heard and valued, they naturally become allies and advocates in building a more diverse workplace.

Mentorship programs are a cornerstone of successful D&I strategies. These programs must be carefully structured to support women's advancement within the corporate hierarchy. By pairing aspiring female leaders with seasoned executives, mentorship provides a framework for growth, guidance, and unlocking potential. Coupled with sponsorship, where leaders actively advocate for women's advancement, mentorship can bridge the gap between latent talent and leadership opportunities.

Another critical aspect of implementing D&I initiatives is to normalize flexible working arrangements. This is not just about offering lip service to work-life balance but about re-evaluating how performance is measured and rewarded. Organisations should focus on output rather than time spent at a desk, offer remote working options where feasible, and recognize that flexibility can lead to enhanced productivity and job satisfaction.

Training is an indispensable element of a successful D&I framework. This goes beyond surface-level diversity workshops and delves into unconscious bias training, conflict resolution, and communication skills workshops. Such programs equip employees with the tools to understand different perspectives and to collaborate more effectively with a diverse group of colleagues and stakeholders.

D&I also means having the courage to confront and quash stereotypes and prejudices when they arise. It's essential to establish a zero-tolerance policy against discrimination and harassment. Creating a safe space for reports of misconduct and following through with fair and transparent investigations underscores a company's commitment to a respectful and inclusive workplace.

Since the corporate world doesn't operate in isolation, it's important to seek partnerships and alliances that can strengthen D&I initiatives. Collaborating with external networks and organizations dedicated to supporting women in leadership can provide valuable resources, perspectives, and momentum to internal efforts.

Moreover, regular assessments and recalibrations of D&I initiatives are vital. Collect data, analyze it, and adjust your strategies accordingly. Acknowledge setbacks as learning opportunities and celebrate successes as stepping stones towards your larger D&I goals. It's through this iterative process that companies build D&I into their DNA, leading to sustainable change.

Empowering employee resource groups (ERGs) that focus on women can also be an effective tactic. These groups can offer strong networks, empowering women through shared experiences, and providing a collective voice to propose and implement gender-specific initiatives.

To solidify institutional memory and normalize inclusive practices, it's essential to document the process and standardize successful approaches. This not only acts as a blueprint for future initiatives but demonstrates to all stakeholders the company's unwavering commitment to diversity and the mechanisms by which it can be achieved.

Lastly, promoting pay equity is a crucial aspect of any D&I initiative. Perform regular pay audits to ensure fairness and address any disparities head-on. Establishing a compensation philosophy that rewards skills, experience, and performance, regardless of gender, sets a clear standard of value and fairness within the organization.

D&I is not an endpoint but a continual journey towards betterment. It's about embedding equity into the fabric of corporate culture and persistently questioning and breaking down barriers that limit women's ascent in the corporate world.

Grounded in the vision that gender should neither hinder nor be a deciding factor for success, the implementation of D&I initiatives can redraw the boundaries of the corporate world, making it an egalitarian space. It's through these steps that companies not only enrich their own diversity tapestry but also contribute to a larger societal shift towards gender equality in leadership roles.

Chapter 17:
Technology and Innovation: Women at the Helm

As we turn the page from diversifying corporate landscapes and inclusive cultures, we anchor ourselves in the dynamic world of technology and innovation, where a cadre of women leaders is forging new frontiers. In a realm where each breakthrough propels us further toward a future rich with potential, women at the helm of tech enterprises are not just participating; they're leading the charge. They're the visionaries crafting pathways in AI, robotics, and green tech, evolving markets, and birthing industries that respond to our most pressing challenges. At this nexus, barriers are viewed not as deterrents, but as invitations to solve and innovate. It's a landscape where creativity meets computation, empathy intersects with algorithmic precision, and diverse perspectives don't just add value—they are essential. As we explore these groundbreaking journeys, we'll see that the infusion of women's insights and leadership styles isn't just transforming the tech industry—it's revolutionising how we engage with the world and with each other, bringing to light technology's most humane and empowering potential.

Emerging Trends

In the ever-evolving corporate landscape, one cannot ignore the transformation that technological advancements have set in motion, especially in the realm of leadership and innovation. As we peruse the pages of history culminating in the digital era, we acknowledge that women's roles in this transformation are not just participants but as trailblazers reshaping the technological and corporate frontiers.

Remote work, once a convenience, is now a staple, providing flexibility that can be leveraged by women juggling their career aspirations with personal responsibilities. The shifting paradigm of work location and hours has altered the corporate environment, allowing for a more inclusive workforce that doesn't penalize career progression for those needing adaptable work arrangements.

Artificial Intelligence (AI) and machine learning are not merely buzzwords. These technologies are carving out new roles and requiring fresh skill sets. Women are now not only consumers of technology but are at the forefront of its development and ethical implementation, ensuring that AI solutions are unbiased and equitable.

Data analytics is another arena where women in leadership can thrive, leveraging their unique perspectives to make data-driven decisions that can transform businesses. With an emphasis on evidence over intuition, this approach can level the playing field in decision-making scenarios traditionally dominated by male perspectives.

Today, we witness a conscious effort towards sustainability in business practices. Women leaders are often seen championing these initiatives, reflecting their intrinsic understanding of the significance of long-term planning and the preservation of resources, not just for the immediate future but for generations to come.

The gig economy is reshaping what employment looks like, offering unprecedented freedom and opportunity for female professionals to pursue their careers on their terms. Women are increasingly taking on freelance roles or forming collectives which afford them agency and flexibility while showcasing their expertise.

Collaborations among diverse groups are being prioritized to fuel innovation. Inclusion drives better business outcomes, and harnessing diverse viewpoints often allows companies to approach problems with more creativity and arrive at more comprehensive solutions.

Digital platforms are providing women with global connectivity, enabling them to learn from, support, and mentor each other irrespective of geographical constraints. These platforms also offer a stage for women to demonstrate their acumen and build influence in their respective fields.

Progress in educational technology has empowered continuous learning and development. Online courses, webinars, and digital certifications are paving the way for women to stay updated with the latest business trends and leadership techniques while managing their careers.

In the realm of entrepreneurship, there is a marked increase in women founding start-ups, particularly in sectors like health tech, educational tech, and e-commerce which often focus on community and quality of life enhancements.

Emerging corporate structures like holacracies are challenging traditional hierarchies. These flatter organizations may provide more opportunities for women to exert influence and impact decision-making processes without the impediments of conventional office politics.

Personal branding through social media has become a powerful tool for aspiring leaders. Women are utilizing platforms such as LinkedIn, Instagram, and Twitter not just to amplify their achievements but also to voice their opinions on industry trends and policies.

With cybersecurity becoming a non-negotiable aspect of business operations, women are stepping into roles that safeguard corporate data and brand reputation. They bring a detail-oriented approach to this field which is vital to outsmarting the sophistication of modern cyber threats.

Lastly, there is a growing wave of cross-sector mobility, with professionals including women leaders transitioning between roles in different industries. This trend breaks down siloes, enriches the talent pool, and allows for the transfer of innovative ideas and practices across industries.

As we dissect these emerging trends, it's evident that the corporate world is standing at the cusp of a revolution. And in this conscientiously evolving ecosystem, women have the potential to emerge as pioneers, steering technological innovation and leadership towards a harmonious and equitable future for all.

Female Pioneers in Tech

The march of progress in technology is relentless, and at its forefront, often unsung, stand female pioneers whose brilliance and persistence break through barriers. Within the silicon heartbeat of our modern age, women have been instrumental in shaping the digital landscape. Their contributions, at times overshadowed by their male counterparts, are critical threads in the tapestry of technological innovation.

Ada Lovelace's early musings on the Analytical Engine laid the groundwork for computer programming, a feat far surpassing the norms of her time. Her legacy endures, reminding us that the potential for groundbreaking ideas does not discriminate by gender. Women like Grace Hopper continued this trajectory, with Hopper's invention of the first compiler acting as a catalyst for software development, a cornerstone of modern technology.

In the halls of contemporaneous progress, the structural steel of binary and code often hears the echo of female determination.

Engineers like Radia Perlman, dubbed the "Mother of the Internet," crafted fundamental protocols that underpin today's digital communications. Their stories aren't just footnotes in tech treatises; they are essential chapters in a saga still being written.

Elizabeth "Jake" Feinler's work was integral in the creation of the internet's domain naming system. Under her leadership, the Network Information Center managed the burgeoning web's directory, a bedrock task for global connectivity. Also pivotal is the story of Shafi Goldwasser, whose work in cryptography ensures the secure transmission of data across a vulnerable cyber world.

We tread amidst a revolution spearheaded by shapers of clay and conduit. The presence of women at the helm marks a potent renaissance, redefining our engagement with the technological world. Such transformative vision is displayed by the likes of Weili Dai, a founding partner of the world's first fabless semiconductor company, who continues to champion diversity in the tech industry.

The digital age is replete with examples of female leadership. Susan Wojcicki took the reins of YouTube and guided it to become an indispensable part of global video-sharing and content creation. Her approach and investments have carved the very architecture of modern digital entertainment and social interaction.

Ensuring a pathway for the next generation, women in tech leadership reinforce the industry's responsibility to encourage girls to pursue STEM subjects. Ginni Rometty, the past CEO of IBM, has been a vocal advocate for including more women in technology fields, driving change not just through her words but by setting IBM upon a course towards full-spectrum diversity.

The quiet labyrinth of cables and screens also echoes with the ascendancy of women of colour, which magnifies the richness of diversity in the corridors of innovation. Kimberly Bryant created Black

Girls Code with the aim of providing young and pre-teen girls of colour opportunities to learn in-demand skills in technology and computer programming, infusing the tech landscape with new perspectives and vitality.

Advocacy for equal representation has found its mark, gleaning results in the form of burgeoning networks of women who support each other's aspirations. These supportive structures demystify technology and present new opportunities for women to conquer. Women Who Code and Girls Who Code are such organisations that drive societal change by hacking the very code of gender paradigms.

At the entrepreneurial frontier, women are not just participants but leaders in technology startups. Innovators like Anne Wojcicki, co-founder of 23andMe, utilise technology not only to create successful business models but also pioneer advances in personalised medicine and genomics, harnessing technology's potential to improve human health and understanding.

The archetype of the technology executive is changing. Gone are the days of homogeneity in the upper echelons of tech companies. Today's female leaders, such as Safra Catz at Oracle, are not only running multi-billion-dollar enterprises but are also dismantling the myth that women don't belong in the boardroom of tech giants.

What emerges is a landscape replete with potential, with the advancement of women in tech a barometer for progress across all sectors. Their stories, marked by perseverance and intellect, aren't anomalies or exceptions. They're emblematic of what can be achieved when opportunity meets talent, irrespective of gender.

Yet, despite these strides, the journey isn't over. For every luminary mentioned, numerous unsung heroines in technological fields remain, facing daily battles against bias and underrepresentation. This reality underscores the crucial need for continued advocacy, support, and recognition of women's role in tech.

The keystrokes of change are persistent. Through forums, panels, and initiatives such as the Grace Hopper Celebration of Women in Computing, the dialogue continues to evolve. These platforms not only document and celebrate the successes of women in tech but also offer insights into overcoming obstacles and advocating for systemic changes necessary for true gender parity.

As we pivot towards the next chapter of corporate evolution, the recognition and empowerment of women in technology will not only be a hallmark of our time, but a beacon for future generations. The legacies of tech's female trailblazers are blueprints for a world where innovation is not constrained by gender, and where the digital future is written in the collective code of humanity, male and female alike.

Chapter 18:
Education and Continuous Learning

The cornerstone of lasting leadership lies in an unyielding commitment to education and continuous personal and professional development. For women striving to ascend the corporate ladder, this pursuit becomes doubly imperative in a dynamic landscape that demands adaptability, strategic acuity and multifaceted expertise. Education doesn't just stop with a degree; it's an expansive bridge that connects experiences, hones skills and fosters innovative thinking. By embracing a philosophy of lifelong learning, women can solidify their roles as versatile leaders, equipped with the knowledge to navigate complex challenges and the wisdom to mentor future generations. This chapter delves into the transformative power of education and offers a compendium of resources designed to elevate a woman's capability to lead with confidence, articulate vision and influence with intelligence. As the business environment evolves, the synthesis of continuous learning with leadership stands not merely as an option, but an imperative for those eager to secure a place at the forefront of change.

Lifelong Learning for Leaders

Lifelong learning is the continuous, self-motivated pursuit of knowledge for personal or professional reasons. As the corporate world evolves, female leaders must focus intently on learning as a continuous journey rather than a destination. Fostering an environment where learning is central to leadership development ensures not only personal growth but also organisational agility in an ever-changing business landscape.

Leadership, while often positioned as an innate skill, is also a craft that can be refined and expanded through continuous learning. It isn't just about attending occasional workshops or completing mandatory training. It means curating an appetite for knowledge, seeking diverse experiences, and integrating learning into the fabric of daily life. For female leaders especially, who may face an array of unique challenges in their careers, the ability to learn and adapt is critical.

Understanding and anticipating market trends, technological developments, and global economics are all central competencies of a successful leader. Such comprehension doesn't flourish in stagnation; it's the result of a concerted effort to keep abreast of changes and digest complex information. Education is more accessible than ever, through online courses, podcasts, industry conferences, and seminars, presenting leaders with endless opportunities for growth.

For women leading teams, it's vital to model lifelong learning behaviours. When a leader shows commitment to her own development, she sets the tone for her team, encouraging them to seek their own growth opportunities. This culture of continuous learning can lead to innovation, as well as more effective problem-solving within a team as multiple perspectives and new ideas are valued and explored.

Also important is the leader's ability to reflect – to look back on experiences and extract lessons. Reflective practice allows leaders to analyse their own behaviours, outcomes of decisions, and team dynamics, leading to improved leadership strategies and interpersonal skills. By encouraging reflection, female leaders can identify areas for personal improvement and set specific learning objectives.

Adaptive learning is another key concept for leaders. This means not just acquiring new knowledge but also unlearning and relearning as the situation demands. Success may often depend on a leader's ability to challenge existing beliefs and adapt to new paradigms. This is particularly poignant for female executives who are pioneering new ways of leading in traditionally male-dominated environments.

The dynamic and sometimes ambiguous roles of leadership necessitate a robust toolkit of skills. Effective leaders must master communication, strategic thinking, emotional intelligence, and a myriad of other talents that are developed and honed through ongoing education. Importantly, these competencies should be aligned with one's personal leadership style, allowing for authenticity in how they are put into practice.

Pursuing formal education such as advanced degrees can be valuable; however, learning should not be confined to structured settings. Informal learning through mentorship, professional networking, and real-life experiences can be incredibly enlightening. Engaging in diverse environments encourages leaders to step out of their comfort zones and exposes them to different ideas and perspectives which can be transformative.

Technology has redefined the approach to learning, with digital resources offering flexibility and accessibility to knowledge. Female leaders have the opportunity to utilise tech platforms to amplify their learning experiences, but it's essential to approach these with a critical mind, seeking sources that are credible and relevant.

Maintaining a balance between professional development and other life responsibilities is another challenge for female leaders. An effective approach to lifelong learning considers the constraints of personal time and energy. Setting realistic goals and integrating bite-sized learning into everyday routines can make the process more manageable and sustainable.

Peer learning is another aspect that should not be underestimated. Sharing experiences, insights, and learnings with contemporaries provides a rich tapestry of collective wisdom that can't be replicated in solitude. For women leaders, participating in or creating forums and networks where knowledge is exchanged not only contributes to their own growth but also elevates the collective knowledge base of female leadership.

As globalisation continues to draw the world closer, it has become imperative for leaders to gain intercultural competency. Familiarity with different cultures, international markets, and global business protocols can all be nurtured through dedicated study and exposure. Female leaders who hone such skills are better equipped to operate on an international stage, a necessity in many high-level leadership roles.

Ultimately, the pursuit of lifelong learning is a deeply personal endeavour that holds different meanings and methods for each individual. Nonetheless, it's clear that for leaders, especially those carving out new paths for women in the corporate world, it's a non-negotiable aspect of their growth and effectiveness. Embracing continuous education as a way of life empowers leaders to not just reach their potential but also to extend the boundaries of what is possible within their organisations and industries.

While this section has underscored the significance of lifelong learning, it also serves as the prelude to practical aspects that will be covered in the subsequent chapters. Educational resources, the importance of health and wellness, promotion strategies, and coping with setbacks are all intertwined with learning and form integral facets of a leader's journey.

Empowering women to lead with confidence and agility hinges on their willingness to embrace learning at every stage of their careers. The landscape of leadership is continuously rewritten, and the leaders who thrive are often those who view their development as an ever-unfolding story rather than a series of achieved milestones.

Educational Resources

In an age where knowledge is power, equipping oneself with the right educational tools can open many doors, especially for those aspiring to leadership. This is particularly vital for women who are navigating the corporate world, where resources tailored to their unique challenges and opportunities can be especially beneficial. In this section, we explore a curated selection of resources aimed at enabling women to fortify their leadership skills, knowledge base, and professional growth.

Let's start with higher education institutions that have taken the mantle in providing executive leadership courses designed for women. These programs often focus not just on honing business skills, but also on addressing specific struggles that female leaders face, such as gender bias and work-life integration. Universities with a rich history of advocating for women in leadership offer these dynamic curriculums, and women can significantly benefit from the specialized training and rich networking opportunities found here.

It's also essential to address the growing number of online courses and webinars that bring these educational experiences right to your desk or even the palm of your hand. These platforms enable learning at one's own pace, which is perfect for busy professionals looking to squeeze in development opportunities in between their commitments. Coursera, edX, and LinkedIn Learning are among the many that provide insightful content across a range of leadership topics, including strategic management, effective communication, and leading with emotional intelligence.

Books, both timeless classics and cutting-edge releases, are an invaluable touchstone for wisdom and inspiration. The market burgeons with literature that dives deep into leadership theories, personal narratives of successful businesswomen, and practical guides on overcoming workplace challenges. These books serve not just as educational tools but also as solace, offering companionship and understanding through shared experiences.

Industry-specific journals and publications offer a window into the latest trends, research findings, and thought leadership in the business world. By subscribing to these periodicals, one can stay well-informed about the shifting landscapes of the corporate world, allowing for strategic adaptive measures to be taken. Harvard Business Review, Forbes Women, and The Wall Street Journal's 'Women In:' series are such examples, providing content that's both informative and enriching.

Conferences, summits, and symposiums focused on women in leadership supply a dynamic environment for education and networking. These gatherings often address topical issues affecting women in the corporate arena, presenting platforms for discourse and opportunities to harness collective knowledge. Notable events such as the Women's Leadership Conference and the Global Women's Forum have become seminal for those wishing to connect and learn from a community of female leaders.

For those looking to address personal development areas, coaches and specialised trainers can provide tailored guidance. By working with a coach, women can focus on specific skills such as public speaking, resilience in stressful environments, and leadership assertiveness. These professionals are adept at helping female leaders uncover their potential and overcome any barriers that may impede their progress.

Furthermore, networking groups and professional associations play a crucial role as educational resources. They often host workshops, training sessions, and provide access to a myriad of resources like white papers, case studies, and policy analyses. These groups foster an environment of knowledge sharing, which is instrumental in the learning process of any leader.

Podcasts and video series dedicated to the subject of female leadership have risen in popularity due to their accessibility and the personal touch they offer. Hearing stories directly from women who have navigated the path of leadership provides real-world insights and strategies that are both relatable and motivational.

Mentorship programs, as discussed in earlier chapters, also double as educational resources. Mentors can impart valuable lessons from their own experiences, providing a living curriculum tailored to the mentee's career aspirations and challenges.

Educational foundations and non-profits focused on gender parity in leadership roles also contribute significantly. These organizations often offer grants, scholarships, and fellowship programs that enable women to pursue academic and professional development opportunities that they may otherwise be unable to afford.

Peer learning circles and mastermind groups should not be underestimated as powerful educational resources. The collective intelligence of a diverse group of professionals can provide multiple perspectives on challenges, offer unique solutions, and reinforce learning through accountability and support.

Lastly, self-directed learning through actions such as job shadowing, volunteering for new projects, and leading initiatives can be incredibly educational. These experiential learning opportunities allow women to apply theory in practice, refine their skills, and build confidence in their abilities.

The landscape of educational resources is as dynamic as it is diverse. With a tapestry of options available, female professionals can craft a learning path that best suits their goals and circumstances. Continual learning is crucial, not just for career advancement but for personal growth and satisfaction. As we move towards an increasingly complex business environment, the appetite for knowledge and the willingness to learn can distinguish the leaders of tomorrow.

These resources provide women with the leverage needed to navigate a professional journey fraught with unique challenges—equipping them with armament for the battles of gender bias, inequality, and underrepresentation. Let us take ownership of our growth and engage with these educational treasures that lie within our grasp, for they hold the keys to enlightened leadership and a more equitable future in business.

Chapter 19:
Health and Wellness for the Busy Executive

As we transition from the empowering insights on continuous learning, we now pivot to a matter just as crucial but often sidelined: the health and wellness of you, the busy executive. In today's fast-paced corporate environment, it's easy to let self-care fall by the wayside, but it's paramount to remember that your well-being is the bedrock of your success. This chapter invites you to consider your health holistically, recognising that peak performance is a blend of physical vigour, mental acuity, and emotional resilience. We'll explore strategies that enable you to prioritise your health amidst a demanding schedule, ensuring that you are as robust in body as you are sharp in mind. From now on, view self-care not as a luxury, but as a non-negotiable investment in your executive toolkit, one that fuels your capacity to lead with dynamism, creativity, and influence. After all, carving out time for wellness isn't a detour from the path to success – it's the very pavement that ensures the journey is sustainable and enjoyable.

Stress Management Techniques

Aspiring and current female leaders face an array of stressors unique to their positions in the corporate world. From navigating a traditionally male-dominated environment to balancing the often-discussed work-life equilibrium, the journey can indeed ignite stress levels that, if not managed, can hamper both wellbeing and performance. It is imperative to equip ourselves with an arsenal of stress management techniques that can fortify us against the pressures that accompany leadership.

Firstly, identification of stress triggers is critical. Awareness of what specifically causes discomfort or anxiety allows the leader to take proactive measures before stress escalates. This could be tightly packed schedules, a particular interpersonal dynamic at work, or even the pressure of decision-making. The objective is not to eliminate these stressors – an unrealistic expectation – but to approach them with a calibrated response that minimizes their impact on our peace of mind.

Mindfulness has become a cornerstone of modern stress management. The practice of being fully present and engaged with the current moment, without distraction or judgement, can foster a sense of tranquility that clashes with the nature of stress. Implementing short mindfulness exercises during the day, perhaps during breaks or in the transition between meetings, can serve as powerful pauses that reset one's emotional state.

Regular physical activity is another potent stress-reliever that is too often neglected amidst hectic leadership duties. Exercise releases endorphins, those natural mood lifters, and helps in shifting focus away from the day's stresses. Whether it's a brisk walk, a yoga session, or a vigorous workout, the key is to find a form of exercise that is enjoyable and thus sustainable in the long term.

Time management strategies can alleviate stress by creating a sense of control and predictability. Effective delegation, prioritization of tasks, and setting realistic deadlines are all part of this approach. It is equally important, however, to carve out personal time in these schedules. Dedicating slots for relaxation, hobbies, and family can rejuvenate the spirit and prevent burnout.

A powerful dialogue that often goes unspoken is the importance of assertive communication in stress management. The ability to communicate needs and boundaries clearly, without aggression or passivity, is essential. Assertiveness can prevent the accumulation of unspoken expectations and resentments that often lead to stress.

Leaders should not understate the significance of a healthy diet in managing stress. Food has the capacity to either soothe or amplify our stress response. A balanced diet rich in fruits, vegetables, lean proteins, and whole grains can provide the consistent energy levels and nutrients needed to cope with the demands of leadership.

Another technique lies in the power of laughter and maintaining a sense of humor. Humor provides a psychological buffer against stress, offering a perspective that can make challenges seem less threatening. Foster an environment that allows for lighthearted moments amidst the seriousness of work.

Building a support network is crucial. Having trusted colleagues, mentors, and friends to share burdens with can alleviate the feeling of isolation that stress often brings. We should not underestimate the power of collective wisdom and the comfort of shared experiences.

Adopting relaxation techniques such as deep breathing exercises, meditation, or progressive muscle relaxation can be quick and effective methods to reduce tension. These can be incorporated into daily routines and called upon in moments of acute stress.

Journaling provides an outlet for processing emotions and stress. Writing down thoughts, experiences, and worries can act as a form of stress release, curbing the intensity of our internal experiences and providing clarity amidst confusion.

It is crucial also to engage in ongoing self-reflection. This can foster resilience by recognizing patterns in one's stress response and tracking improvements over time. Self-reflection enforces personal accountability and growth by confronting challenges with a constructive lens.

Embracing a growth mindset is also fundamental when managing stress. Perceiving challenges as opportunities for learning and development rather than threats can transform the energy associated with stress into motivation and innovation. This mindset shift can decrease anxiety and promote a proactive approach to problem-solving.

Lastly, sleep cannot be neglected. High-quality sleep recharges the mind and body, equipping leaders with the energy and mental clarity to tackle stress. Prioritising sleep is, thus, a non-negotiable strategy in stress management.

In our relentless pursuit of progress and equality in the corporate sphere, stress can emerge as a stealthy foe. By adopting a range of stress management techniques custom-tailored to our unique needs and leadership roles, we fortify our resolve and maintain our wellbeing. The effectiveness of such strategies is not just in their adoption, but in their consistent application. As leaders, let us champion not just the success of our businesses, but equally the health and wellness of ourselves and those we lead. Our ability to manage stress is tantamount to our capacity to lead with excellence and pave the path for the generations of female leaders who will follow in our footsteps.

Physical and Mental Health Priorities

As leaders, it's vital to acknowledge that success is not solely measured by professional achievements but by how well we manage our physical and mental health. Prioritising health is not a luxury—it is a necessity that plays a critical role in the longevity and quality of one's career, especially for women who may face unique health challenges. Integrating health-conscious practices into daily routines is essential.

Regular fitness activities can prevent burnout, enhance cognitive function, and improve overall well-being.

One of the key aspects of maintaining physical health is to ensure a balanced diet. The food consumed can be as influential as any business strategy. Nutrient-rich foods fuel the body, leading to better energy levels and higher work performance. As busy executives, it's easy to fall into the trap of convenient but unhealthy food options, however, planning and conscious choices can make healthy eating a seamless part of a hectic schedule.

Leaders must not underestimate the power of quality sleep. Sleep is the foundation upon which a resilient leader is built. Lack of sleep affects decision-making, creativity, and can lead to serious health consequences over time. While the corporate world often hails those who burn the midnight oil, leaders should set an exemplary culture by promoting adequate rest as a pillar of success.

Just as crucial as caring for the body is attending to one's mental health. Mindfulness and meditation have been shown to decrease stress levels, enhance emotional intelligence, and aid in maintaining focus. In a landscape where decisions often come with high stakes, a clear and centred mind is one of the most potent tools a leader can possess.

Leaders should not shy away from seeking professional help when necessary. Therapy or counselling sessions can be instrumental in navigating through work stress, providing new perspectives, and fostering better coping mechanisms. This proactive approach to mental well-being is commendable and should be normalised within the corporate environment.

Another element crucial to a leader's health is the ability to disconnect. The digital age has blurred the boundaries between work and personal life, making it more important than ever to establish clear limits. Time away from the screen allows for rejuvenation and may lead to higher productivity when re-engaging with work tasks.

Humour and laughter inherently have therapeutic effects. They not only reduce stress levels but also help in bonding with teams, creating a more positive work environment. Leaders should embrace opportunities for levity, remembering that a lighthearted moment can cut through tension and foster a spirit of camaraderie.

Equally significant are social connections and relationships. Investing in personal relationships can create a support network that is invaluable during times of stress. Whether it is family, friends, or peers, these bonds offer comfort and can be grounding, reminding leaders of life outside the corporate sphere.

Recognising the signs of burnout is imperative. Burnout can manifest in exhaustion, a lack of enthusiasm, and reduced professional efficacy. Leaders need to be vigilant about these symptoms, both in themselves and their team members, and take preemptive steps to address the issue.

Exercise is not only a means to maintain physical fitness but also a potent stress reliever. Whether it be a brisk walk, a yoga class, or a session at the gym, finding an exercise routine that is enjoyable can lead to consistency and, consequently, better health outcomes. Moreover, incorporating team-building activities that involve physical exercises can promote a culture of health within the organisation.

Women leaders must also be mindful of specific health screenings and check-ups that are essential at various life stages. Regular medical appointments should not be overlooked, regardless of how demanding the work environment may be. Preventive care is the most straightforward step towards longevity in one's career and life.

Leaders should advocate for health and wellness initiatives within their organisations. By doing so, they not only address their welfare but also set a standard for their teams. Health benefits, wellness programs, and mental health days are all examples of how companies can foster a culture that prioritises well-being.

It is crucial to personalise health and wellness strategies. What works for one individual may not work for another. Hence, leaders should be open to exploring and finding what best aligns with their lifestyle and needs.

Lastly, balancing professional demands with personal health entails accepting that perfectionism is a myth. Leaders must learn to set realistic expectations for themselves, understanding that it is okay to ask for help and delegating tasks when necessary. Productivity should never come at the cost of health.

In conclusion, physical and mental health priorities are not separate from the journey of leadership—they are integral to it. The strategies for maintaining health are as diverse as the challenges that leadership presents. By embracing the importance of health and actively integrating wellness practices into daily life, leaders not only enhance their performance but also model a sustainable path to success for those they lead.

Chapter 20:
Scaling the Ladder: Promotion Strategies

As we've navigated the nuanced terrain of challenges and catalysts for women in leadership, it's crucial to turn our attention to a practical roadmap for ascending to higher tiers of corporate hierarchy. In 'Scaling the Ladder: Promotion Strategies', we delve into the complex choreography of climbing the career ladder, focusing on actionable guidelines that demystify and streamline the promotion process for women. We'll understand that knowing when and how to position oneself for career advancement isn't just about ambition—it's about strategic planning, thoughtful career trajectory plotting, and a keen sense of timing. Acknowledging the often subtle nuances that affect women differently in the workplace, this chapter empowers you to craft a tailored approach that resonates with your professional aspirations. From leveraging your unique value proposition to the fore, to articulating your achievements and aspirations effectively, it's about shaping your narrative to create an undeniable case for your advancement. We'll explore methods to enhance visibility within an organisation and decipher how to navigate the unspoken rules that often govern promotional considerations—ensuring you're not just ready for the next step, but that others can't help but invite you to take it.

Understanding the Promotion Process

As we turn the page to "Understanding the Promotion Process," we delve into the intricacies of corporate advancement and the unwritten rules that significantly affect women's upward mobility. A focused understanding of the promotion process is paramount for anyone intent on climbing the corporate ladder.

At its core, promotion is not just about being competent or diligent in one's role. While these are important facets, promotions are deeply rooted in visibility, networking, and strategic positioning within an organisation. Women, particularly those with leadership aspirations, must navigate a complex matrix of performance, politics, and perception to realise their career progression goals.

Firstly, to commandeer the pathway to promotion, one must excel in their current position. Exceeding expectations and showcasing exceptional performance is the bedrock of promotion eligibility. It's crucial to understand that leadership roles are typically filled by those who demonstrate a track record of results and reliability. Thus, it's essential to document achievements and contribute to projects that have a tangible impact on the company's bottom line.

Despite the meritocratic ideal, promotions often involve an element of subjective evaluation. Sponsorship is a critical factor in this regard. A sponsor, unlike a mentor who advises, actively champions and advocates for your promotion within the organisation. Cultivating relationships with influencers and decision-makers can open doors that performance alone may not.

The complexity of the promotion process is heightened by unconscious biases that can cloud judgement. Gender biases can result in women being overlooked for leadership roles or certain projects that are critical for advancement. To mitigate this, women must be proactive in communicating their ambitions and ensuring that their contributions are recognised and associated with their names.

The concept of executive presence also plays a significant role. This is often an amalgamation of confidence, communication skills, and professional demeanour that convinces others you're ready for leadership. It involves a fine balance, especially for women, who may be unfairly judged as too assertive or not assertive enough.

Understanding organisational politics is another essential aspect. It's about more than just doing your job well; it's also about navigating the power dynamics and aligning oneself with the right projects and people. These politics can sometimes be subtle, and other times overt, but they are always a reality in the journey to the top.

Another consideration is the timing of promotions. There are often specific cycles or seasons when organisations look at promoting individuals. Understanding these cycles and preparing for them by showcasing your achievements and readiness for increased responsibility can increase your chances of being considered for promotion.

Additionally, articulating your value and potential can sometimes be overlooked. Self-promotion, in a tactful and professional way, is necessary so that the value you bring to the organisation is not just known, but top-of-mind when leadership roles become available.

For women in the workplace, tackling stereotypes about leadership abilities is an ongoing struggle. Research shows that women are often perceived as less suitable for leadership roles due to biased perceptions about gender and leadership. It's critical to dismantle these stereotypes not just through dialogue but by presenting a counter-narrative through solid achievements and leadership acumen.

Furthermore, the promotion process should be seen not as an isolated event but a continuous journey of career development.

Seeking feedback, engaging in professional development activities, and being open to lateral moves that expand one's skill set can all be part of this process. These actions tell a compelling story of growth and readiness for the next challenge.

Securing promotion also requires strategic career planning. This means not only excelling in one's current role but also developing skills and experience for the next level. Understanding the prerequisites for advancement and actively working towards them positions you as a natural successor when opportunities arise.

Women should also be aware of the potential for burnout during this process. It's essential to recognise the importance of work-life balance and self-care. Burnout can stall even the most promising career trajectory. Therefore, maintaining the energy and passion needed for leadership is as critical as professional accomplishments.

In summary, understanding the promotion process involves a mixture of excelling in one's current role and mastering the often subtle art of corporate dynamics. It requires a strategic approach to relationships, a robust showcase of achievements, and an awareness of the timing and politics of promotion. Moreover, it demands resilience, as the journey is fraught with challenges unique to women in the workforce.

As this discussion sets the stage for the subsequent sections that will focus on more specific strategies and actions, remember this foundation. The mastery of the promotion process is not just about climbing a ladder but about successfully navigating the maze of talents, relationships, and opportunities that define the corporate landscape.

Planning Your Career Trajectory

As you forge ahead in your professional journey, it's imperative to strategise and map out your career trajectory with precision and foresight. The corporate landscape may seem like a labyrinth, but with a clear plan in hand, the path to success can become more navigable. By consciously developing your career trajectory, you set yourself up not just for progression, but also for fulfilling your potential as a transformative leader in the business realm.

The first step in planning your career trajectory is to reflect deeply on your values, interests, and strengths. Understanding what drives you and where your competencies lie makes it easier to pinpoint opportunities that align with your professional ethos. It also helps in articulating a personal mission statement that serves as a beacon throughout your career. This statement isn't just a slogan; it's a promise you make to yourself, an anchoring force amidst the ever-changing dynamics of corporate life.

It's vital to then market yourself for future opportunities, ensuring that your capabilities are visible to those who matter. This involves building a robust professional profile that highlights your achievements and potential. Update your CV regularly, craft a compelling LinkedIn profile, and showcase your accomplishments through measured self-promotion. Remember that visibility in the workplace isn't solely about being seen; it's about being recognised for your value and contributions.

Setting specific, attainable goals with realistic timeframes is the framework of a well-thought-out career trajectory. Short-term objectives keep you motivated and focused while long-term ambitions anchor your ultimate professional aspirations. However, be flexible; as new opportunities and challenges arise, you may need to revisit and revise your goals to reflect the evolving business environment and your personal growth.

Within your trajectory, it's important to target roles that stretch your ability and force you out of your comfort zone. Each position should be a building block, granting you a new set of skills and experiences that pave the way for your next move. Avoid stagnation at all costs, because the comfort of the known can be the enemy of growth. Embrace change as it comes and harness it to fuel your ascent up the corporate ladder.

Networking is an essential ingredient in planning your trajectory. Foster meaningful relationships within and outside your industry as these connections often lead to opportunities and insights that can prove invaluable. Don't underestimate the power of a diverse network—the wider the range of your contacts, the broader your perspective and knowledge base will become.

Mentorship, similarly, is a critical aspect of career planning. Seek mentors who have travelled the path you aspire to tread. A mentor provides guidance, opens doors, and often acts as a sounding board for your ideas and decisions. Form multiple mentoring relationships to gain a multifaceted understanding of various leadership styles and strategies.

As you aim for the next rung on the career ladder, it's beneficial to take charge of your professional development. This might involve further education, certifications, or skill-building workshops that augment your existing expertise. Lifelong learning signals to current and prospective employers your commitment to being at the forefront of industry knowledge and leadership trends.

Understanding organisational dynamics is another key point of focus. Observe and analyse how decisions are made in your organisation, who are the key influencers, and what criteria and performance indicators matter most. This knowledge will empower you to position yourself effectively for promotions and to contribute to strategic discussions.

Volunteer for leadership roles in high-visibility projects or committees within your organisation. These roles allow you to demonstrate your potential as a leader and can be a powerful component of your career planning strategy. They also give you a chance to work cross-functionally, which is critical for understanding the holistic picture of how your organisation operates.

Self-awareness is crucial in planning your career trajectory. Regularly seek feedback on your performance and leadership style, using this information to refine your approach and strengthen your interpersonal skills. Building emotional intelligence is just as important as expanding your technical knowhow in becoming an effective and respected leader.

Risk-taking is inherent in any career trajectory that aims for growth. Calculated risks can lead to significant rewards and set you apart from your peers. Embrace the unknown with confidence and resilience, knowing that even if you face setbacks, these experiences will sharpen your decision-making abilities and possibly open unexpected doors.

Be proactive in seeking opportunities, rather than waiting for them to come to you. Keep an eye on internal job postings, industry trends, and potential positions that align with your career path. Tailor your approach and pitch yourself as the best candidate for the role. This assertive stance can help you control the direction and flow of your career.

Finally, while plotting your career trajectory, balance ambition with authenticity. Stay true to your principles and don't sacrifice your integrity for advancement. Ambition is commendable, but without a grounded sense of self and a genuine respect for others, it can lead to a hollow victory. There's a strength in cultivating a leadership style that's compassionate, collaborative, and centered on adding value.

As you chart your course through the business world, keep in mind that your trajectory is uniquely your own. There will be moments of triumph and times of trial, but throughout it all, the power to shape your career—and by extension, the corporate culture—rests with you. Embrace the responsibility wholeheartedly, and you'll find that your journey not only elevates your standing but also paves the way for others to follow.

Chapter 21:
Coping with Failure and Setbacks

Even the most successful among us know that the path to leadership is never devoid of stumbling blocks. In this chapter, we delve into the crucial skill of resilience—a trait as invaluable as strategic thinking or adept decision-making. You'll discover how to channel your inner strength to confront disappointments head-on, how to distil valuable lessons from experiences that did not culminate in triumph, and how to emerge from adversity with a renewed sense of purpose. This narrative isn't about the glorification of setbacks; it's about equipping you with the fortitude to acknowledge them, learn from them, and pivot accordingly. Practical wisdom shared in this chapter will guide you to craft a personal blueprint for resilience, tailor-made to your leadership journey, fostering a mindset that views every setback not as the end but as an integral part of the learning curve leading to a more robust, indomitable you.

Resilience in Leadership

In the preceding chapters, we've explored an array of skills and strategies that equip women to ascend the echelons of corporate leadership. Now, let's delve into a trait that is paramount yet often understated: resilience. The path to leadership is fraught with challenges, and for women, these are compounded by historical and cultural barriers. Resilience, therefore, becomes not just desirable, but essential for the modern female leader.

What exactly is resilience in the context of leadership? It's the ability to persevere in the face of setbacks, to maintain focus on objectives despite adversity, and to recover from failures with renewed purpose. For women leaders, resilience is what fuels the drive to break glass ceilings, challenge biases, and embody the change they wish to see in their organizations.

One may wonder why resilience is considered a gendered issue. The landscape of business has been traditionally male-dominated, a terrain where women have had to assert their right to participate and lead. This historical context has cultivated a requirement for greater resilience among women leaders, for not only must they navigate their professional challenges but also the cultural and systemic biases that seek to restrain their rise.

How then can resilience be fostered? It begins with mindset. A growth mindset, as opposed to a fixed mindset, allows leaders to view challenges as opportunities for development rather than insurmountable obstacles. It is a perspective that embraces learning and views effort as a pathway to mastery. Women leaders who adopt this mindset can reframe setbacks as stepping stones to success.

Resilience also involves emotional intelligence. Women leaders who can manage their emotions and navigate the emotions of others with empathy and understanding are better positioned to sustain morale and inspire their teams through tough times. Emotional intelligence acts as a buffer against the stress that often leads to burnout. It's about maintaining composure and projecting confidence even when situations are volatile.

Beyond mindset and emotional management, a practical approach to building resilience involves calculated risk-taking. Confronting risks and emerging on the other side, irrespective of the outcome, builds the psychological muscle required to withstand future challenges. Women in leadership positions need to normalise risk-taking as part of their role, encouraging themselves and others to step out of comfort zones and embrace the unknown.

Support networks play a crucial role in resilience, too. The saying 'no man is an island' holds especially true for women in leadership. Building relationships with mentors, peers, and support groups provides a safety net that women can depend on for advice, encouragement, and a sense of community. These networks are both a source of strength during difficult times and a platform for sharing strategies and stories of overcoming adversity.

Another dimension of resilience is maintaining a healthy work-life balance. This equilibrium allows women leaders to recharge, keeping burnout at bay and ensuring they return to their professional challenges with vitality. Personal well-being is inseparable from professional endurance, and leaders must prioritise self-care as part of their resilience-building regimen.

Resilient leadership encompasses the nurturing of a positive organisational culture. A culture that encourages transparency, values employee well-being, and celebrates even the small victories creates an environment where resilience thrives. Leaders must champion these values, embedding them into the DNA of their companies to build teams that are robust in the face of adversity.

Anticipation and preparedness are further facets of resilience. By anticipating potential issues and having contingency plans in place, women leaders can navigate setbacks more smoothly. Preparedness does not necessarily prevent challenges, but it does ensure that leaders are not caught off-guard and are equipped to deal with problems swiftly and effectively.

The communication of resilience cannot be overlooked. Women leaders must articulate their vision with conviction, even during times of uncertainty. Clear communication instils confidence in their teams and stakeholders, and it is here that persuasive and motivational skills are pivotal. In articulating the way forward, leaders solidify their own resolve and energise those around them.

Continuous learning is integral to resilience. The most effective women leaders are those who are lifelong learners. They constantly seek new knowledge, insights, and skills that enable them to adapt and grow. In an ever-evolving corporate landscape, this adaptability ensures that they can weather changes and emerge as innovators and disruptors.

But what of failure? Resilient leaders understand that failure is not the opposite of success; it is part of the journey towards success. Women who lead fearlessly know that failures are not to be shied away from but to be analysed for the rich lessons they provide. These leaders are adept at bouncing back from failures, using them to inform better strategies and decisions in the future.

Ultimately, resilience in leadership is about legacy. Paving the way for future generations of women leaders means demonstrating that challenges can be overcome and that adversity can be a catalyst for growth and success. It's about setting an example that instils courage and fortitude in those who will follow.

So, resilience is more than just a tool; it's a hallmark of transformative leadership. As we continue to work towards gender equality in the corporate world, let's remember that the resilience of today's women leaders is not only shaping their personal leadership journeys but also carving out paths for the female executives of tomorrow.

Learning from Loss

Amidst the often-championed narratives of success and ascent in the corporate world, the journey of learning from loss stands conspicuously critical yet frequently overshadowed. Loss, be it in the form of a missed promotion, a failed project, or the dissolution of a business venture, harbours profound lessons essential to the growth and fortitude of a leader. For women in leadership, understanding how to harness these experiences can transform potential setbacks into meaningful growth opportunities.

Contrary to the cultures that celebrate only achievements, the texture of loss adds depth to one's professional persona. The ability to dissect a loss and extract actionable insights is one that distinguishes extraordinary leaders from their counterparts. Women, who are often scrutinized more critically, must especially learn to use failure as a stepping stone rather than a stumbling block.

The first poignant step in learning from loss is acceptance. It is human to feel despondent when faced with disappointment, but acceptance empowers you to move beyond the emotional response. Acknowledging a loss provides the foundation needed to analyse the situation objectively without being clouded by defensiveness or denial.

Reflection follows acceptance. By engaging in thoughtful analysis, you can uncover the root causes of the loss. This introspection should be thorough and brutally honest—ask yourself what could have been executed differently, recognize any warning signs that were missed, and identify the decisions that led to the end result. It is through this lens of self-awareness that a leader starts constructing the scaffold for future triumphs.

For a woman in a competitive environment, it is particularly crucial to separate constructive criticism from gendered bias when analysing loss. Understand that some factors will be beyond your control, including inherent biases in the workplace. However, focus on those aspects that can be managed and improved upon. Doing so not only propels personal growth but also sets a precedent for handling loss with grace and professionalism.

Building resilience is another integral aspect of learning from loss. This quality is what enables leaders to bounce back from setbacks with renewed energy and perspective. Resilience doesn't entail sheer grit but also encompasses the flexibility to adapt to changing circumstances and the wisdom to pivot when necessary. Crafting this resilience personally paves the way for fostering resilient teams as well.

Never underestimate the power of mentoring during times of loss. A mentor can offer not just emotional support, but an external perspective that can help you see the bigger picture. Mentors have often weathered similar setbacks and can share invaluable advice on turning loss into a learning opportunity.

Moreover, treating every loss as a case study is a potent way to enrich your leadership toolkit. Dissecting what went wrong, scrutinizing every decision, and understanding the dynamics at play turns mere experience into applicable knowledge. This methodical approach instills a proactive mindset towards tackling future challenges.

It's also important to communicate openly about failures. In doing so, you contribute to a culture where loss is recognized as part of the growth process. Sharing your learnings with peers and team members can cultivate an environment of trust and continuous improvement. Remember, transparency can be a powerful leadership attribute.

Learning from loss also necessitates a shift from a fixed mindset to a growth mindset. The latter thrives on challenges and perceives failures not as evidence of unintelligence or lack of capability but as heartening springboards for development and for honing one's abilities.

When faced with loss, it's vital to maintain perspective. While it's important to take the lessons to heart, it is equally essential not to equate a professional setback with a personal deficiency. Balance critique with compassion, allowing yourself room to grow without being harsh or unforgiving. After all, leadership is as much about personal compassion as it is about professional rigor.

Furthermore, documenting your journey through loss can be therapeutic as well as instructive. Penning down your experiences, the lessons learned, and the strategies for moving forward not only aids in solidifying these lessons but may also serve as guidance for others when published or shared, emphasizing the fact that loss is universal and can be a conduit to remarkable leadership maturity.

A crucial lesson from loss is learning to redefine success. Success in leadership doesn't always align with upward progression; sometimes it's about broadening your skill set, deepening industry insights, or strengthening your resolve. By recognizing this, female leaders can create a more diverse and authentic definition of what it means to succeed.

In the wake of loss, it's equally imperative to set new, achievable objectives. The act of planning entails both the courage to look forward and the determination to apply what has been learned. Strategic goal setting transforms the intangible insights gained from loss into concrete steps on the pathway to achievement.

Lastly, embracing loss as an integral part of the narrative changes how it's perceived—not as an endpoint, but as a chapter in a larger saga of leadership. For women, integrating these experiences into one's leadership journey is a testament to resilience, adaptability, and the indefatigable spirit that characterizes true leadership.

In conclusion, while the discourse of ascending to and thriving in leadership roles often highlights victories, learning from loss is an equally critical chapter in a leader's growth. For women, who may navigate more complex corporate terrains laden with biases and unique challenges, the capacity to turn loss into a potent source of learning is not just important—it's essential. Turning the pages from setbacks to comebacks, the lessons learned become the undercurrent that drives future success, validating the notion that, indeed, every loss is an unopened gift in the realm of personal and professional development.

Chapter 22:
The International Arena:
Women in Global Leadership

As we expand our horizons from the national to the global stage, women in leadership are breaking new ground, shaping international affairs with finesse and unmistakable skill. The ascent of women to positions of power on the global platform is not simply about occupying seats at high-stakes tables; it's about the insightful integration of diverse cultural contexts into the strategic fabric of global businesses. Women leaders, with their unique propensity for empathy and collaboration, are adept at navigating the subtle nuances of cross-cultural relations, often turning potential conflicts into opportunities for innovation and shared success. Within this chapter, we delve into the dynamic realms where these leaders operate, unearthing the challenges they encounter, from language barriers to differing societal expectations, and celebrating the mosaic of triumphs that women have crafted across continents. We explore the quintessential role that adaptability, cultural intelligence, and inclusive leadership play in not just overcoming these barriers, but in forging a path that others may follow. The narrative of women in global leadership is not just one of overcoming, but one of redefining success on an international scale, binding the professional sphere with threads of inclusivity, cultural respect, and mutual growth.

Cross-Cultural Challenges

As we venture into the international realm of leadership, it becomes increasingly important to navigate the intricate mosaic of cultural intricacies. For women executives, the undertaking is not just about transcending geographic boundaries but also about understanding and adapting to diverse cultural norms and practices that define the world of business. Embracing this diversity can unlock doors to global opportunities, yet it brings to light the cross-cultural challenges that can significantly shape a leader's journey.

Cultural competence is not merely an asset; it's a foundational pillar for women who aim to lead effectively across different cultural contexts. It's about recognising that what works in one culture might not translate well into another. Leadership styles, communication patterns, and even the way success is measured can vary dramatically from one region to another. You, as a leader, must be attuned to these variations to lead with empathy, efficacy, and understanding.

One of the most prevalent issues faced by women in global leadership is the varying degrees of gender equality around the world. In some cultures, female leaders are a norm and widely accepted, while in others they may be a rare sight, facing intense scrutiny and resistance. This disparity can manifest in overt discrimination or in subtler ways, such as through ingrained societal attitudes and unconscious biases that undermine women's authority and competence.

To navigate such complexities, it's critical to cultivate local knowledge. This means understanding the historical and cultural context that shapes business practices and workplace interactions. It's about learning the nuances of communication, from the explicit to the implicit messages conveyed in different settings. Are decisions made in hierarchical or egalitarian fashions? Is direct or indirect communication the norm? Addressing these questions is paramount in cross-cultural environments.

Language barriers, too, pose significant hurdles. Mastery or proficiency in the local language enhances credibility and allows for deeper connections with colleagues, partners, and clients. However, even if you can't be fluent, showing respect and making an effort to learn and use elements of the local language can go a long way in establishing rapport and trust in a new cultural landscape.

Understanding the local approach to work-life balance is another aspect of navigating cross-cultural waters. Varied cultural expectations about workplace presence, the acceptability of discussing personal life in professional settings, and the boundaries between the two can significantly impact the approach women leaders must take in different countries.

Women in global leadership roles often need to be champions for diversity and be conscious of how they themselves may have internalised gender norms. Being a role model means challenging stereotypes not just at home but also abroad, and using one's position to foster more inclusive environments for other women in the organisation and in the industry at large.

Furthermore, cross-cultural negotiation tactics require an understanding of the local value systems. This involves recognising what is prioritised and respected in each culture, be it time, relationships, or process, and adapting negotiation strategies accordingly. Here, the female leader's ability to read the room and the cultural cues becomes invaluable.

As we continue to advance in our global leadership roles, fostering an international network becomes a lifeline. Strong networks can offer support, advice, and local insights that are essential for navigating the cross-cultural chopping waters. They also serve as a platform for advocacy, driving change towards more equitable and accepting business environments worldwide.

Relocating to a new cultural setting doesn't just impact business decisions; it affects personal life tremendously. The support a leader receives from their family and the company when moving internationally can greatly influence their effectiveness and well-being in the new role. Organisations should hence be proactive in providing integrative assistance to their executives taking on global positions.

Dressing the part is another subtle, yet potent, form of communication. Attire that aligns with local norms can be an expression of respect and an understanding of cultural customs. For women, finding the balance between professional attire and cultural sensitivity can sometimes be a nuanced affair.

In the face of all these challenges, it's essential not to lose sight of one's authentic leadership style. Being adaptable and culturally sensitive doesn't mean you should forsake your unique approach to leadership—it's about finding the intersect between your authenticity and cultural alignment that resonates with a global team.

Success in global leadership also calls for emotional intelligence—understanding one's emotions and those of others, and managing them within the tapestry of cultural expectations. High emotional intelligence allows you to connect with people from diverse backgrounds and to lead with compassion and clarity, allowing for differing viewpoints and expressions of thought.

Investing in cross-cultural training is not just beneficial; it's a strategic imperative. Guided by experienced facilitators, such trainings can prepare emerging leaders for the demands of operating in multiple cultural contexts, providing them with the tools and strategies needed to succeed.

Lastly, learning from other women who have traversed the path of international leadership before us can offer valuable insights. History is dotted with women who have not only survived but thrived in complex cross-cultural scenarios, and their stories of perseverance and adaptability can serve as powerful lessons for the current and next generation of female leaders.

As women continue to rise through the corporate ranks and take on international leadership roles, understanding the cross-cultural challenges and strategically navigating through them becomes central to leadership excellence. It's a journey of continuous learning, adaptability, and resilience, but one that heralds the progression of women's indelible impact on the global business landscape.

Success Stories from Around the World

As we turn our gaze across the global corporate stage, a mosaic of progress regarding women in leadership unfolds. While barriers persist, there's also a spirited push for gender equality that has given rise to a cadre of formidable female executives. Their narratives are not only tales of personal triumph but also templates for dismantling the structural impediments to women's professional ascent. As we explore success stories from around the world, we're reminded that the capacity for change resides within all realms of possibility when ambition is matched with opportunity.

In Europe, the ascent of women to top executive roles is heartening, exemplified by the tale of a Swedish executive who spearheaded digital transformation in a leading telecommunications company. Her approach, centred on inclusive leadership and team empowerment, drove performance and fostered an enviable organisational culture. Her story is proof positive that collaborative environments can yield exceptional results, setting a benchmark for others to follow.

Across the Pacific, in Japan, a country grappling with deeply ingrained gender norms, the rise of the first female CEO of a major automobile manufacturer is a testament to the winds of change. Her journey was marked by strategic risk-taking and visionary leadership, culminating in her pioneering work with electric vehicles. As a trailblazer in a traditionally male-dominated industry, she's rendered the glass ceiling a concept to be shattered, not just cracked.

In Africa, where economic diversity varies widely, women leaders are emerging with robust solutions to regional challenges. A Ghanaian entrepreneur, for instance, has garnered international acclaim for her innovative agribusiness model, empowering local farmers and championing sustainability. Her approach harmonises economic acumen with social responsibility, illustrating that leadership is as much about uplifting others as it is about individual success.

Moving to the Middle East, despite cultural hurdles, a female fintech founder from the United Arab Emirates has made strides in a sector where women are markedly underrepresented. Her platform has revolutionised online payment systems, enhancing the region's economic infrastructure. This disruptive innovation challenges the status quo and exemplifies the transformative power of women in technology.

In Latin America, a Chilean businesswoman has redefined the mining industry's leadership paradigm with her commitment to environmental stewardship and ethical practices. As a CEO, she has proven that profitability and sustainability can coexist, propelling her company to the forefront of green mining initiatives.

In North America, a narrative of triumph is found in a Canadian tech entrepreneur who has excelled in a realm where women are often sidelined. She has broken new ground with her software enterprise, championing diversity and equal representation in tech roles. Her success is emblematic of the potential unlocked when inclusive recruitment and career progression policies are embraced.

In Oceania, Australian women are at the forefront of innovation in renewable energy. One notable leader's commitment to eco-efficient technologies has placed her clean energy startup on the global map. Her business acumen and passion for sustainability serve as a blueprint for future female entrepreneurs in the green tech space.

Reflecting on these narratives, one discerns certain commonalities – resilience in face of adversity, a willingness to challenge industry norms, and a palpable vision for a more equitable future. Each leader's journey underscores the multiplier effect of fostering diversity in leadership: it propels innovation, drives economic growth, and cultivates a fairer societal ethos.

Surely, these stories of triumph reach beyond personal accolades; they are emblematic of collective progress. They eschew the notion that gender parity in leadership is an unattainable ideal, instead reinforcing the reality that female leaders are not just succeeding but excelling worldwide. These achievements offer not just inspiration but a pragmatic blueprint for dismantling gender biases and building a world where leadership is defined by talent and tenacity, not gender.

These anecdotes of success also compel us to reassess our own biases and expectations surrounding female leadership. They exemplify a profound truth: that transformative leadership knows no gender. It is a mosaic built on the strength of diverse experiences and perspectives. Each story adds a crucial piece to the puzzle, highlighting unique strategies that have enabled these women to excel in their respective fields.

With these global success stories, we witness a convergence of culture, creativity, and courage. They encapsulate the spirit of our times, where the pursuit of equality is intertwined with the quest for excellence. The strides made by these pioneering women are not merely incremental; they are foundational, laying the groundwork for generations of women leaders to come.

To aspiring female leaders, these stories are veritable treasure troves of wisdom. They serve as both a lantern in the dark and a mirror reflecting the readers' own potential. They galvanise us to persevere through challenges, to innovate within our spheres of influence, and to relentlessly pursue our vision of success.

In closing, the narratives shared in 'Success Stories from Around the World' may differ in geography, industry, and culture, but they all share a unifying thread - the transformative impact of women in leadership. As we herald these inspiring tales, we must continue to forge pathways that enable women from all corners of the world to rise to the apex of leadership. Their successes are not isolated phenomena but beacons of progress for all who strive for a world where gender equality in corporate leadership is not an aspiration but a reality.

Chapter 23:
Legislation and Policy: The Path to Equality

In our journey toward crafting a world where gender does not define one's professional ceiling, we arrive at the powerful intersection of legislation and policy—crucial mechanisms for levelling the playing field for women in leadership roles. This chapter delves into the intricate tapestry of laws and regulations that have been enacted to support women's ascent in the corporate realm. It outlines the current legal frameworks that protect and enhance women's career opportunities, whilst also shedding light on areas where advocacy can catalyse much-needed change. The evolution of gender equality is partially orchestrated by our ability to translate social ideals into concrete, enforceable standards that hold institutions accountable. You, as a reader immersed in the quest for corporate leadership equality, are invited to scrutinise these instruments of change, understand the role they play in your journey, and envisage how you might influence policies that pave roads to empowerment for future generations of women leaders.

Laws Affecting Women Leaders

As we delve deeper into the realm of female leadership, it's vital to recognise the legal scaffolding that supports or hinders the ascension of women into positions of power. While the corporate world may sometimes present itself as a meritocratic space, the intricacies of law play a pivotal role in either levelling the playing field or perpetuating systemic inequities. In this section, we explore the legal barriers women leaders often face and the strides taken by legal systems worldwide to mitigate these issues.

The journey of legal reform concerning gender equality began earnestly in the latter half of the 20th century. At this juncture, governments around the world started to codify equal rights, recognising the critical contribution of women to all aspects of society. One such landmark legislation is the Equal Pay Act, initially established in many countries to prohibit wage discrimination based on sex. Despite these measures, the gender pay gap persists, subtly evolving in ways that law sometimes struggles to keep pace with.

Anti-discrimination laws, such as those encapsulated within the Equality Act or Title VII of the Civil Rights Act in some countries, were heralded as transformative. Designed to prevent discrimination in the workplace on various grounds, including sex, these laws provided a foundation for women to challenge unfair treatment and bias. However, the interpretation and application of these laws in real-world scenarios have often been fraught with challenges, necessitating continual advocacy and legislative updating.

Harassment in the workplace, a plight disproportionately faced by women, has been another focal point for legal systems. Laws like the Sexual Harassment Act have aimed to create safer work environments by holding harassers and their employers accountable. Compliance and enforcement, however, remain significant hurdles, underscoring the need for a holistic approach that extends beyond legal remedies to transform workplace culture.

Family leave policies also directly influence the trajectory of women in leadership positions. The provision (or lack thereof) of maternity leave, paternity leave, and parental leave can dictate a woman's ability to return to her career after having children, impacting her chances of advancing to leadership roles. Progressive laws that provide comprehensive, paid family leave are fundamental in supporting women as they balance their roles as both leaders and caregivers.

Quotas and affirmative action laws have been implemented in some regions to tackle the representation gap in leadership positions. They are often seen as a controversial yet necessary measure to catalyse change in entrenched corporate structures. Critics argue that such interventions can undermine meritocracy, yet proponents point to the substantial progress in countries with these provisions, highlighting the role of law as a catalyst for social change.

With technological advancements and the digital transformation of businesses, new laws concerning privacy, cyber harassment, and online discrimination have become increasingly important. Women leaders in the tech industry, in particular, must navigate complex legal challenges that were unimaginable a few decades ago. Legal literacy in these areas is becoming non-negotiable for those who wish to safeguard their reputation and the well-being of their organisations.

Intellectual property laws also hold special significance for female leaders, especially for those in creative, tech-driven, or innovative fields. Ensuring that the fruits of one's ingenuity are protected by law is paramount, and women must be equipped with the knowledge to assert these rights and the means to defend against infringement.

Corporate governance laws additionally affect how women can influence an organisation's strategic direction. Requirements for board diversity, disclosure of gender pay gaps, and transparency in recruitment practices are increasing in various jurisdictions. Such governance-related laws aim not only to promote diversity but also to foster an environment where equitable leadership can thrive.

When considering international leadership roles, women must also grapple with varying legal landscapes. Laws relating to business conduct, expatriate work permissions, and international labour standards vary widely. Understanding and complying with these can be a make-or-break factor for female leaders aiming to succeed on the global stage.

Financial and securities laws can disproportionately impact women who aim to break barriers in industries such as banking and finance. Regulations defining permissible conduct, investment practices, and disclosures have significant implications for those leading financial institutions. Women's progress in these sectors is often contingent on understanding the intricate web of financial regulation across different markets.

Health and safety laws form an often overlooked but critical aspect of the environment that women leaders operate within. Ensuring that workplaces meet the standards required for women's health, including but not limited to reproductive health, is an area where the law has a profound impact on maintaining a diverse working population and a critical consideration for women in positions of influence.

Considering the ascendancy of women in the legal profession, gender-specific legislation affecting women lawyers and judges has gained relevance. From inclusive dress codes to protocols around maternity and flexible working, women in this field must contend with and shape the law to create spaces conducive to their success.

Finally, it's crucial to address laws regulating political activity and civic engagement. Women leaders, particularly those who are active in advocating for legislative changes, must navigate these laws to effectively voice concerns about gender equality and influence policy. Challenges such as campaign financing laws, lobbying regulations, and political representation impact how women can leverage their leadership roles to effect change on a greater scale.

To summarise, the landscape of laws affecting women leaders is a testament to the strides made towards equality and the journey yet before us. Each legal victory is a hard-fought chapter in a larger narrative of progress. Aspiring and existing women leaders must be acutely aware of these laws – to utilise them as tools for growth, and to advocate for those that pave the way to a more equitable future in leadership.

In the next sections, we'll look at how advocacy plays a pivotal role in furthering this agenda and ensuring that laws continue to evolve in step with society's ambitions for gender equality in leadership.

Advocacy for Change

Advocacy isn't merely a tool at one's disposal; it is the linchpin in our collective journey towards a more equitable corporate world. Aspiring and established female leaders alike recognise the importance of advocating for policy changes that create an environment ripe for gender equality. To manifest this change, one must adopt a stance of proactive engagement, fostering open dialogue and pushing for legislative reforms that close the gender gap.

First and foremost, it's critical to understand the legislative landscape and the factors influencing gender inequality in the business realm. It's not uncommon for women to encounter systemic hurdles, whether it's imbalanced maternity leave policies or tax laws that inadvertently favour a single-earner household—a nod to outdated gender roles.

To challenge this status quo, informed advocacy begins with mastering the intricacies of existing laws and policies. Women must join forces to pinpoint the legal barriers holding them back, collaborating with legal experts to dissect complex legislation and lobbying policymakers for meaningful change.

Let's consider the machinations of advocacy. It may be strategic, involving structured campaigns designed to target specific policies or utilising platforms to draw attention to pressing issues. Change-makers can use their voices to articulate the case for parity in board representation or the abolishment of practices that perpetuate the pay gap.

Moreover, advocacy thrives when it's a collective movement—uniting women across hierarchies and industries to champion a common cause. Power lies in numbers, and a united front amplifies our ability to enact change. Networking not only builds connections but also reinforces solidarity amongst women pushing for policy reforms.

Why does advocacy matter? Because it has the potential to influence the fabric of our society, moulding the architecture of the workplace for future generations of women. Engaging in advocacy builds awareness, generates support, and catalyses action, embedding the principles of diversity and equality in corporate governance.

It's worth examining successful advocacy campaigns to distil elements that can be replicated. Thoughtful tactics, like targeted advocacy on social media or harnessing the power of public petitions, have proved effective in engaging stakeholders and promoting corporate responsibility.

In the quest for balanced workplaces, male allies are also indispensable. Encouraging men to become advocates for change is transformative. When men in leadership champion gender equality and co-sponsor necessary policy changes, they lend invaluable support to the cause. Their voices add credibility and urgency, countering resistance and helping to dismantle the patriarchy that often pervades corporate culture.

Furthermore, consider timing and cultural nuances. Advocacy efforts should coincide with moments when public and political will is most receptive. Aligning with broader social movements or using data to drive home the economic benefits of gender equality often elevates the effectiveness of advocacy campaigns.

Real movement, however, goes beyond mere lip service. It is essential that advocacy translates into concrete steps within the corporate environment. Training programmes to identify unconscious bias, developing fair recruitment practices, and transparently reporting gender metrics are practical starts to institutionalising change.

International perspectives bring additional complexity to advocacy. Women's rights are not monolithic, and understanding regional variations in gender equality is vital. Advocacy strategies must be adaptable and culturally sensitive, recognising diversity within the tapestry of women's experiences worldwide.

One can't overstate the importance of legal advocacy groups and NGOs dedicated to the cause. These organisations possess the expertise and clout to push for legislative changes at national and international levels. Allying with these bodies enhances one's potential to influence policy and galvanise public opinion.

As we preach the gospel of advocacy, we must not forget the role of education. Enlightening society about gender inequality and its repercussions fortifies the foundations of advocacy. Educational initiatives, whether in formal institutions or through corporate training, are as much a part of advocacy as lobbying and campaign work. They are long-term investments into the mindset of the next wave of business leaders.

What about the personal aspect of advocacy? It materialises when female leaders leverage their positions to advocate for others. This can mean supporting junior colleagues or debating policy at the executive table. In every interaction, there is an opportunity to foster an ethos of equality and inclusivity.

And so, the march towards true gender equality in the corporate sphere continues—with advocacy as its standard bearer. It is a nuanced art, an informed strategy, and an impassioned plea for a world where women stand equal to their counterparts. Every voice raised, every policy challenged, and every stereotype shattered paves the way for a future where female leadership isn't the exception, but the norm.

Chapter 24:
The Future of Female Leadership

The tide is shifting with a palpable force as the canvas of female leadership evolves, beckoning an era where possibility intertwines with tenacity to carve out new paradigms. Envisaging the future, we see a tapestry of gender-diverse boardrooms flourishing with the innovative perspectives that women bring to the fore. Visionaries not only foretell trends; they are the genesis of uncharted glories, illuminating paths for burgeoning female thought leaders. Preparing the next generation for the landscape that beckons requires both resolve and strategic foresight, empowering them with adaptive skills, technological proficiency, and a deep-rooted sense of global citizenship. It's this transformative power of female leadership—interwoven into corporate DNA—that promises to redefine industries, galvanize change, and manifest a future where leadership bears the indelible imprint of gender equality.

Predicting Trends

In the ever-evolving corporate arena, predicting trends is akin to forecasting the weather in a complex climate system. As we harness the collective wisdom and scrutinise the trajectories of different industries, we gain insight into the forces shaping the future of female leadership. In this chapter, we'll discuss these emergent patterns and how they will influence the ascent of women in business roles across various sectors.

One key trend we are witnessing is the global acknowledgment of diversity as not just a moral imperative but a business one. Investors and stakeholders increasingly recognise that diverse leadership teams correlate with enhanced innovation and better financial performance. Companies leading the way in gender diversity are setting precedents and benchmarks for others to follow, creating a ripple effect across industries. This is a trend that seems poised not only to continue but to escalate in the coming years.

Technological proficiency will increasingly become a critical component of leadership effectiveness. As technology propels industries into new realms of operation, women at the helm must be conversant in these tools and trends. This doesn't mean that every leader must be a tech wizard, but it does require an understanding of the implications and opportunities that technology presents. This includes embracing digitisation, artificial intelligence, and data analytics – areas that offer enormous potential for innovation and strategic advantage.

The traditional career trajectory is shifting. A somewhat linear path to leadership is becoming less prescriptive and more fluid. We're starting to see careers that blend different disciplines, roles, and industries as advantageous, particularly for women who often juggle multiple responsibilities. Rather than a hindrance, a varied career path can be a source of strength and resilience, imbuing leadership with a breadth of perspective that's valuable in a rapidly changing world.

As we look to the horizon, the role of mentoring and sponsorship is set to increase substantially. The wisdom of those who have navigated the labyrinth of corporate advancement will be more critical than ever. We predict that organisations will institutionalise mentorship programs and networks, creating structured pathways to support women's progression towards leadership roles.

Work-life integration will remain a hot topic, as the quest for balance becomes ever more complex in a hyper-connected world. While technology has blurred the lines between office and home life, it has also created opportunities for flexible work arrangements. Companies that provide genuinely flexible working policies will be at the forefront of attracting and retaining top female talent.

Another trend that has emerged with increasing clarity is the importance of self-care and wellness in leadership. Executives are now expected to sustain high performance over lengthier careers. Those organisations that foster an environment that prioritises mental and physical health will see their leaders—both male and female—thrive.

In the financial realm, gender-lens investing is gaining traction. This type of investment strategy, which focuses on funding businesses that benefit women or that are led by women, is expected to flourish, guided by evidence that such ventures often yield strong returns. This has the potential to alter the investment landscape and provide additional capital to innovative companies championing gender equality.

Transparency in gender equality metrics will become standard as shareholders, employees, and consumers demand more robust accountability. As a result, we foresee that companies will not only publish annual reports on gender diversity but also set concrete, measurable goals for improvement. This transparency will provide an impetus for change and a compass for assessing progress.

The way companies approach maternity and paternity leaves will also likely undergo considerable re-evaluation. Progressive companies are already offering more equitable policies to support families, and this will become increasingly common as businesses recognise the retention and morale benefits of such support.

Within the realm of corporate governance, we expect to see a steady increase in female representation on boards. Legislative changes, shareholder pressure, and a plethora of research outlining the benefits of diverse boards will ensure that boardroom composition continues to progress towards gender parity.

Social and environmental responsibility will also become a core component of corporate strategy, largely influenced by female leadership. Women leaders are often seen as more empathetic and socially conscious, traits that align well with the growing public expectation for companies to exhibit corporate social responsibility. This development is likely to lend itself to a world in which leadership that values sustainability and ethical practices is not just celebrated but demanded.

In the educational sphere, we'll see an expansion of programmes specifically tailored to foster leadership skills in women. These will range from executive education courses to mentor-led training initiatives. Life-long learning will be central to adapting to new challenges and technologies, and women will need to be proactive in seeking out these resources.

Finally, let's reflect on the legal and policy environments that create a foundation for gender equality. While progress here can often seem painfully slow, there is a global movement towards stronger legislation that supports equality in the workplace. This ranges from equal pay legislation to anti-discrimination laws and quotas for women in senior roles. Harnessing this momentum requires continual vigilance and advocacy, alongside strategic action within organisations.

In conclusion, the future of female leadership is irrefutably tied to the acknowledgement that when women succeed, businesses and societies flourish. On the crest of this truth rides the next wave of leaders—women eager and ready to take the helm, women who will not only predict these trends but shape them. Recognising, preparing for, and driving these trends will be an integral part of building a legacy of inclusivity, innovation, and leadership excellence.

Preparation for the Next Generation

Investing in the future signifies not just planning for our own careers, but also nurturing and laying the groundwork for the generations that will follow. As female leaders, we shoulder a unique responsibility to kindle the aspirations of the young women who will inherit the corporate world after us. Doing so involves a commitment to fostering an environment that promotes equal opportunities and nurtures talent irrespective of gender.

Encouraging the next generation begins with communication – open, honest, and inspiring dialogues about the possibilities that await. Young minds are malleable, and our words can either light the path to leadership or reinforce the old barriers that we have worked so hard to dismantle. Share success stories, challenges overcome, and the grit that paved the way; telling these narratives instils confidence and the belief that they too can make their mark.

Gone are the days when leadership was a distant, untouchable concept for young women. Role modelling is essential, and it takes form in everyday situations – at home, within schools, and in the workplace. When young girls and women witness leadership in action, especially by those they can identify with, it normalises female authority and capability; it suggests a world where their dreams are not just mere possibilities, but realities waiting to be seized.

Educational institutions play a pivotal role in the grooming of potential leaders. It's crucial that these establishments go beyond textbook knowledge – instead, spearheading initiatives that build leadership skills. As business professionals, engaging with local schools and universities to offer mentorships, workshops, and internships to young women equips them with firsthand experience and invaluable insights into the business world.

Mentorship creates a direct bridge between experienced executives and the next generation. While finding a mentor is central to personal growth, being a mentor is equally significant. As mentors, we provide guidance, challenge assumptions, and help mentees navigate the intricacies of corporate dynamics – all while celebrating milestones and instilling the resilience needed to tackle setbacks.

Exposure to practical experiences is just as vital as academic preparation. Encourage internships, not as mere resume fillers, but as opportunities to understand the real-world application of academic concepts, develop professional networks, and gain a clearer vision for their own career paths. These early forays into the business environment present learning opportunities that no classroom can replicate.

Women have long been underrepresented in certain strategic business roles, particularly those related to STEM fields. To prepare the next generation, we must actively promote these career paths, dispel the myths that pervade them, and support educational programmes that make these subjects accessible and exciting for young women. This is not just about creating a pipeline of talent, but about changing the narrative of what women can accomplish.

Investing in leadership programmes specifically tailored for young women can also make a substantial impact. These programmes must address the unique challenges that women face in the corporate environment while highlighting the importance of building resilience and authenticity in one's leadership style. Workshops that tackle issues such as negotiation tactics, public speaking, and self-promotion empower young women with skill sets that are often overlooked in traditional education.

Succession planning is an area that can often be more intuitive for women, given our intrinsic understanding of legacy and nurturing growth. In the corporate context, this means identifying potential leaders early and crafting individual development plans that align with their strengths and aspirations. By doing so, organisations not only secure their future leadership but also send a powerful message that they are invested in their female employees' growth.

Networking isn't just for the established; it's a critical tool for aspiring leaders, too. Facilitating connections between young talent and seasoned professionals provides a platform for learning, visibility, and access to opportunities that might otherwise be elusive. Encourage young women to join and participate in professional networks, attend industry events, and seek out connections that align with their interests and goals.

Beyond business competencies, it's imperative that young women understand the value of personal branding. They must be conscious of how they present themselves, their work ethic, and their contributions. This doesn't mean altering their personality to fit a mould but understanding the interplay between perception and professional advancement. Workshops focused on personal branding can provide insights into how to curate a presence that aligns with authentic leadership.

Acknowledging the importance of self-care and well-being is also necessary to prepare the next generation for the trials of leadership. Burnout and work-related stress are real concerns in today's fast-paced corporate world. Encouraging young women to balance professional ambitions with personal health will ensure they have the longevity and vitality to lead effectively and with compassion.

Legislation and corporate policies are continuously evolving, and staying abreast of these changes is essential for upcoming leaders. We can empower the next generation by providing them with knowledge and understanding of employment laws, women's rights in the workplace, and the impact of policies on gender equality. This legal acumen will equip them to advocate for themselves and others, shaping a fairer corporate landscape.

As we look ahead, we're not merely passing the baton; we're strengthening it, embedding it with our wisdom, our courage, and our experiences. Preparing the next generation of female leaders is a testament to the progress we've made and a beacon for the strides yet to come. It's a commitment we make – a promise to the future that their journey will not only be possible, but it will be supported, celebrated, and welcomed with open arms.

Chapter 25:
An Action Plan for Aspiring Female Leaders

Transitioning from a vision of equitable representation in the upper echelons of business to a tailored strategy for personal ascent, this chapter unfolds a practical blueprint for the ambitious woman set on shattering the proverbial glass ceiling. Recognizing that intention without a plan is but a wish, it's incumbent upon the go-getters to delineate their objectives with clarity and resolve. The cornerstone of this action plan must respect individual career aspirations while fostering a systemic approach to professional growth, ensuring that aspiration dovetails seamlessly with pragmatic execution. Focus will be on setting strategic, achievable goals that resonate with one's core competencies and align with wider industry movements, thereby positioning oneself at the cutting-edge of leadership trends. Thriving in the current business climate necessitates both foresight and adaptability—a duality that this action plan embodies, steering clear of the granular, to instead reinforce the tenacity and agility required to navigate and embrace the complexity of ascending the corporate ladder.

Goal Setting

As we turn the page on the challenges and stereotypes that have been previously discussed, let's delve into the essence of goal setting—an instrumental facet of crafting an impactful leadership journey. Napoleon Hill once said, "A goal is a dream with a deadline," a notion that captures the pragmatic beauty of goal setting. For aspiring and current women leaders, setting precise, ambitious goals is not just a roadmap to success; it's a declaration of intent, a commitment to transformation, and the basis of a strategy that challenges the status quo.

First and foremost, we must recognise that goal setting is no mere list making; it's an art that balances ambition with the practical scaffolding required for attainment. Goals aren't abstract wishes; they are the measurable milestones upon which you will plot your career trajectory. Effective goals challenge you to stretch beyond your comfort zone, yet they remain concrete, actionable, and time-bound.

For women in leadership, goal setting takes on additional dimensions. Goals must reflect not only career aspirations but also personal values, seeking a synergy between the two that can sometimes seem elusive. This requires both introspection—understanding what truly matters to you as a leader—and an outward strategic vision that can identify opportunities in your environment.

Setting goals also inherently involves an understanding of the landscape. Being aware of the unique hurdles faced by women in leadership positions is one element, but so too is the current industry climate within which one operates. Goals should accommodate both the reality of these external pressures and the unyielding personal commitment to progress and performance.

While setting goals, it's vital to employ a granularity of approach: long-term ambitions are vital, but they are achieved through the cumulative effect of short-term objectives. These shorter goals often form a 'step-ladder', where each rung represents an incremental move towards the zenith of one's ambitions. However, it's not just about climbing; sometimes, goals can be about consolidation, ensuring stability and sustainability within your current role before seeking to ascend further.

Specificity in goal setting cannot be overstressed. Vague targets are the harbingers of failure. Precisely defined goals, conversely, provide clear benchmarks for success. This clarity transforms the nebulous into the tangible, grounding one's aspirations in reality, and facilitating realistic strategies for their achievement.

Goal setting is an ongoing process, not a one-time event. As you achieve one set of goals, new ones must emerge to replace them. These shouldn't simply be iterations of past goals but should reflect an evolving career and personal growth. This is the 'stretch' element of goal setting that prevents complacency and ensures that aspirations continue to advance and inspire.

Within the quest for leadership success, one must also be vigilant about potential internal and external barriers to goal attainment. Recognising and strategising around these barriers is essential. Whether it's overcoming self-doubt, breaking through middle-management plateaus, or navigating organisational politics, the goals set should come with a realistic appraisal of what it will take to surpass these hurdles.

Moreover, the setting of professional goals should not exist in a vacuum, separate from personal goals. Indeed, for sustained success and wellbeing, one must seek harmony between the two domains. Professional goals that undermine personal well-being or values are ultimately self-defeating. Compassionate goal setting that honours one's whole life is critical for long-term success and fulfilment.

Accountability is an essential companion to goal setting. This starts with self-accountability: monitoring progress, celebrating achievements, and recalibrating when necessary. Yet, having an external support system can also be incredibly beneficial. Whether it's a mentor, professional coach, or a peer network, having others to hold you accountable to your goals can make the crucial difference between aspirations and realities.

Flexibility, too, is a characteristic of effective goal setting. While goals ground us, they should not be so rigid as to restrict our potential. The capacity to adapt goals in response to changing circumstances or new information is a sign of pragmatic leadership. This adaptability must, however, remain directed and not lead to continuous goal shifting which can undermine overall progress.

Visualisation is a powerful tool in the goal-setting arsenal. Envisioning not only the outcome but also the path to that outcome can create a mental and emotional blueprint which guides behaviour and decision-making. It turns the abstract goal into something real and attainable in the mind, thus embedding commitment to its pursuit.

Goal setting, ultimately, is about continuous personal and professional development. It's about setting a legacy and having a transformative impact on both one's life and the lives of others. Effective goals are those that inspire and provoke growth, foster resilience, and contribute to the collective rise in women's leadership.

As we approach the end of this conversation on goal setting, remember this: without a target, there can be no triumph. The act of setting goals is an assertion of your potential and your purpose. It's an embrace of possibility and a foundational step towards crafting a leadership narrative that not only shatters glass ceilings but also builds new skies in which to soar.

With the pathway to achievement now drawn out in the context of goal setting, the following chapter will guide you through the execution and follow-through necessary to transform these goals from vision to reality. They say that well-begun is half done, and with your goals now set, you're already on your way to carving out your distinct legacy in the corporate world.

Execution and Follow-through

In the preceding chapters, we've navigated the historical context of women's ascension in the business world, scrutinised the myths surrounding the glass ceiling, dissected leadership styles, and devised strategies for fostering mentorship, communication, and executive presence. Now, as we approach the zenith of the action plan for aspiring female leaders, we must anchor our ambitions in the profound discipline of execution and follow-through.

In the lexicon of leadership, many a word waxes lyrical on vision and planning, yet it's the execution that transmutes potential into milestones. For a female leader, mastering this art becomes not just a choice but a career-defining imperative. Execution is the enactment of strategy, the breath of life into objectives — a process through which ideas are transformed into reality. It's where the rubber meets the road, crystallizing insights into outcomes.

You may have delineated your goals with meticulous precision, but without an unwavering commitment to execution, these remain but dreams. Follow-through is your steadfast companion along this journey, ensuring that no stone is left unturned, no effort is spared in the relentless pursuit of excellence. It is the sustained effort after the initial thrust, the sense of responsibility towards completion.

An effective execution strategy starts with prioritisation. As professionals juggling multiple roles, women must discern where to allocate time and resources, applying effort where impact is maximised. What tasks will move you closer to your objective? What milestones are critical to your progress? Prioritisation isn't merely about making to-do lists; it's about making to-do lists work for you.

Acknowledge, too, the merit in setting incremental targets; breaking down colossal goals into manageable tasks that are achievable within shorter time frames. It enables monitoring progress, adjusting strategies timely and keeping motivation aflame with the warmth of small victories.

But setting targets isn't enough. To truly excel in execution, one must cultivate a mindset of persistence and determination. It's often the grind after the excitement of a launch that determines success. This persistence is fuelled by a passionate belief in one's goals and an unwavering vision of the end result.

Communication here, too, asserts itself as an indispensable ally. As you execute, ensure clarity in your directives and feedback. Effective leaders articulate their actions, share their progress, and inspire their teams to march alongside them with shared conviction.

Simultaneously, execution is an art that thrives amidst adaptability. A market fluctuates, an unforeseen challenge arises, or a strategy falters — the executive woman poised for success is one who can pivot with agility, refine her approach and steer her ship through tumultuous waters with a composed hand. Rigidity can be the silent saboteur of execution; embrace fluidity, and you embrace growth.

Accountability stands at the pulpit of execution. It is not enough to delegate; one must follow-up, evaluate and take ownership of both victories and setbacks. As a leader, model this accountability, take charge of outcomes and demonstrate a commitment to not just initiate, but to complete.

Use technology and tools to your advantage. Automate where possible, employ software to track progress, and let data illuminate the path of your strategy's success or need for adjustment. Technology is the astute executor's companion, alleviating burdens and sharpening precision.

In follow-through lies another subtle art — that of acknowledging and celebrating your team's contributions. A leader who recognises efforts ensures a team that's engaged and inspired to push through challenging phases. Cultivate a culture of appreciation, it forms the bedrock of a resilient, results-oriented team.

Moreover, effective execution and follow-through demand discipline. Stay true to your deadlines, maintain high standards for your work, and instil within your team a sense of timely completion. Discipline is the silent drumbeat to which success marches.

It's also crucial to conduct reviews and reflections at each stage of execution. Evaluate what's working and what isn't, ascertain the effectiveness of your strategies, and allow feedback to refine your approach. This cycle of action, assessment, and adjustment keeps you aligned with your goals.

At times, execution will be testing, demanding from you more patience and tenacity than you thought possible. In these moments, recall that a leader's mettle is forged in the fires of perseverance.

Last, don't fear to iterate. Your first execution plan may not be flawless, and that's alright. With each endeavour, your mastery of execution and follow-through will sharpen. It's an evolutionary process, one that polishes your leadership to a brilliance that's uniquely yours.

As this chapter closes, carry forward the conviction that while vision sets the direction, it's execution and follow-through that will take you across the finish line. The business world awaits the imprint of your achievements, the stories charted not just by goals, but by the relentless drive towards their realisation.

Chapter 26:
The Continuing Quest for Gender Equality in Leadership

As we reflect upon the rich tapestry of information and insights woven throughout the preceding chapters, it's evident that the quest for gender equality in leadership is not merely a subplot in the grand narrative of our professional lives — it is the very heart of it. This journey is marked by the breathtaking landscapes of progress and the steep cliffs of remaining challenges. Yet, the ascent continues, fuelled by determination, hard-fought gains, and the transformative potential of inclusive leadership.

Progress in the world of business and corporate leadership has been incremental, but it is undeniably ongoing. The history of women in business is not a relic of the past but a backdrop against which we measure today's strides and triumphs. Past milestones serve as the foundation for present trends, establishing a legacy that empowers current and future leaders.

The glass ceiling, once considered an impenetrable barrier, now shows cracks and fissures, evidence of the collective efforts to redefine leadership norms. These myths and realities highlighted in our discussions challenge us to persevere, to push beyond the metaphorical barrier and envisage a workspace truly reflective of equality.

Much has been deliberated about the distinct leadership styles traditionally associated with gender. The juxtaposition of female and male perspectives offers a blend of strengths that can enhance company culture and performance. It is clear that leadership efficacy transcends gender; the focus must be on leveraging these differences to create a dynamic and versatile leadership landscape.

The role of mentorship and networking has emerged as a cornerstone for success. By finding mentors and building robust networks, women can navigate the tumultuous seas of corporate advancement with surer, more confident strides. These relationships form a lattice of support, invaluable for both personal growth and professional development.

In the fight against bias and stereotypes, a strategic approach is needed to identify and counteract the prejudices that often go unchallenged. Women in leadership must continue to employ strategies that break down these barriers, proving through action and achievement the fallacy of such limiting beliefs.

The concept of work-life balance has evolved from a mythical ideal to a tailored harmony. Case studies of successful balances illustrate that personal and professional satisfaction need not be mutually exclusive. Crafting this equilibrium remains a personal undertaking, yet it's vital for sustainable career success.

Self-promotion, often perceived as a tightrope walk between confidence and humility, remains a key skill for women in the pursuit of leadership. Mastering the art of visibility ensures that accomplishments don't go unnoticed and that the value brought to the table is recognized and rewarded.

Support from family, friends, and even foes plays an undeniable role in shaping a woman's career trajectory. The complexities of these relationships can both propel and challenge one's progress, underscoring the need for a supportive ecosystem that reinforces rather than undermines leadership ambitions.

Effective communication and negotiation skills emerge as equalizers in the workplace, arming women leaders with the necessary tools to assert influence and achieve favorable outcomes. Assertiveness, paired with strategic negotiation capabilities, enables voices to be heard and respected.

Executive presence, while often elusive, has been demystified to some extent, revealing the components—such as gravitas—that can be nurtured and developed. Cultivating this presence is a continuous process, one that women can strategically enhance to project confidence and authority.

While women have undoubtedly made inroads in male-dominated industries, the path is often laden with unique challenges. The triumphs celebrated within these spheres serve as powerful examples of what can be achieved when determination meets opportunity.

The pay gap remains one of the most stubborn indicators of inequality. Understanding this disparity is only the first step; deploying tools for negotiating equal pay is crucial for closing the gap and asserting the economic value of female leadership.

Women's roles in corporate governance have become increasingly prominent, foreshadowing a future where board representation is not just tokenistic but powerfully influential in shaping policy and culture. This progress marks the dawn of a more egalitarian corporate governance era.

Entrepreneurship stands out as a beacon of opportunity, a frontier where women are not just participating but leading the charge. The entrepreneurial mindset fosters innovation and growth, revealing the boundless potential when women take the helm of their business ventures.

Finally, let this be a clarion call, not to a finite victory but to the ongoing march towards a future where gender equality in leadership is not the aspiration but the norm. The baton is passed to you, the steward of this mission, as we continue, side by side, in the relentless pursuit of equitable leadership — for the today and the many tomorrows to come.

Appendix A: Resources for Female Executives

Empowering women in leadership positions requires more than just a desire for change; it's about equipping oneself with the right tools, information, and networks to navigate the corporate landscape effectively. This appendix is a curated selection of resources specifically tailored to female executives. From professional associations to educational programmes and more, the resources listed here can serve as valuable means to bolster your career trajectory and help you leave a lasting impact in your industry.

Professional Organisations and Networks

Connecting with like-minded professionals can offer a wealth of support, mentorship opportunities, and career insights:

Women in Management: A global organisation dedicated to supporting women in leadership roles across all sectors, providing training, networking, and mentorship.

Female Executives Network: A networking group for senior women executives, focused on sharing best practices, leadership strategies, and personal growth.

Global Women's Leadership Network: A diverse organisation aimed at empowering women worldwide to assume leadership positions and effect change on a global scale.

Educational Programmes

Continuous learning is pivotal for staying ahead in today's dynamic business environment:

Executive Leadership Programmes: Many top universities offer executive education programmes tailored for women, designed to refine leadership skills, strategic thinking, and organisational influence.

E-learning Platforms: Accessible and flexible, online platforms such as Coursera or edX provide courses on executive leadership, finance, negotiation, and other key business topics.

Online Portals and Publications

Stay informed with the latest research, opinion pieces, and articles concerning women in business:

Harvard Business Review - Women at Work: A podcast series and publication on gender and the workplace, offering insights from successful business leaders and researchers.

The Female Lead: An online platform filled with stories and case studies highlighting the diverse and transformative roles of women in business and society.

Events and Conferences

Attending events can not only broaden your knowledge base but also expand your professional connections:

Worldwide Women's Leadership Conferences: These events focus on global trends affecting women in leadership, offering a platform for networking, inspiration, and collective action.

Annual Female Executive Summits: Many regions host annual gatherings for women in executive roles to discuss challenges, share solutions, and highlight successes.

Mentoring Programmes

Mentorship is a critical component for career advancement, offering guidance, support, and opportunities to learn from others' experiences:

International Mentoring Networks: Engage with a global community of women leaders available to mentor and support your journey to executive leadership.

Peer Mentoring Groups: Local or industry-specific groups provide platforms to exchange experiences with peers who can relate to, and advise on, your career challenges and ambitions.

The path to leadership is multifaceted and these resources are by no means exhaustive, but they're a strong starting point. As a female executive, it's vital to invest in yourself, your skills, and your network. Harness these resources to not just thrive but also to drive change and champion gender equality in the corporate sphere.

Glossary of Terms

The journey towards the pinnacle of corporate success is often paved with terminology as rich and varied as the experiences that define it. Grasping the essence of these terms can not only enhance your understanding but also empower you in both conversation and action. With clarity, let us delve into the lexicon that shapes the discourse on gender equality within the corporate theatre.

A

Affirmative Action - A policy favouring those who tend to suffer from discrimination, especially in relation to employment or education.

B

Bias - An inclination or prejudice for or against one person or group, particularly in a way considered to be unfair.

Board Representation - The presence of individuals on a company's board of directors, representing different stakeholders.

C

Ceiling Effect - A situation where the level of progression or advancement is artificially limited.

Corporate Governance - The system of rules, practices, and processes by which a company is directed and controlled.

D

Diversity & Inclusion (D&I) - A strategy and practice to include diverse individuals who bring various perspectives and backgrounds to a professional environment, ensuring all have equal access to opportunities.

Digital Ceiling - The barriers that exist for women trying to rise to the top in the technology sector.

E

Equal Pay - Compensation that indicates men and women are paid equally for equal work and experience.

Executive Presence - The ability to project confidence, poise, and assertiveness in a corporate leadership role.

G

Glass Ceiling - An unofficially acknowledged barrier to advancement in a profession, particularly affecting women and minorities.

Gravitas - Dignity, seriousness, or solemnity of manner; an important and decisive quality in business leadership.

L

Leadership Styles - The different approaches and strategies employed by leaders to motivate and manage teams.

M

Mentorship - The guidance provided by an experienced person to a less experienced one within a professional setting.

N

Negotiation Skills - The ability to successfully influence discussions and achieve mutually beneficial results.

Networking - The action or process of interacting with others to exchange information and develop professional or social contacts.

P

Pay Gap - The difference in remuneration between two groups of people, exemplified by the gender pay gap.

Promotion Strategies - Tactics and plans to advance one's career within a corporate structure.

R

Resilience - The capacity to quickly recover from difficulties; toughness.

S

Self-Promotion - The action of promoting or publicising oneself or one's activities.

Stereotype - A widely held but fixed and oversimplified image or idea of a particular type of person or thing.

Stress Management - Techniques and strategies to control a person's levels of stress.

Succession Planning - A process of identifying and developing new leaders to replace old leaders when they leave, retire, or die.

T

Tokenism - The practice of making only a perfunctory or symbolic effort to be inclusive to members of minority groups, especially by recruiting a small number of people from underrepresented groups to give the appearance of equality.

This glossary serves as a beacon for navigating the labyrinth of terminology associated with corporate leadership and gender equality. With each term, you're equipping yourself with the knowledge and vocabulary to contribute meaningfully to conversations and, indeed, to the broader cultural change needed within the corporate world.

Appendix B:
Interview Transcripts with Female Leaders

In the pursuit of understanding the nuances of female leadership across different sectors, we've had the privilege of engaging with trailblazing women who've carved a niche for themselves amidst a challenging corporate landscape. The candid conversations encapsulated in these transcripts highlight the passion, resilience, and innovative spirit shared by these female frontrunners. They provide a rich trove of advice, sharing their journeys, the obstacles they've navigated, and the strategies they've employed to surmount them.

Interview 1: Jane Doe, CEO of Innovatech Ltd.

Q: Jane, what's been the most significant barrier in your career?

A: Initially, it was breaking into a male-dominated tech industry. The scepticism was palpable, but I focused on providing undeniable value and let my work speak for itself. It's all about building credibility and maintaining a strong professional ethic.

Q: Can you share a strategy that helped you in your leadership journey?

A: Sure. The most powerful tool for me was cultivating a support network both inside and outside of the industry. This network isn't just to rally around successes; it's there to provide diverse perspectives and invaluable support during challenging times.

Interview 2: Sarah Tan, Chief Financial Officer at Globex Corporation

Q: Sarah, has mentorship played a role in your ascent to CFO?

A: Absolutely. Having a mentor to guide me, especially one who's traversed similar hurdles, was instrumental. But I also learned to mentor myself, in a way, by constant self-reflection and challenging my own decisions.

Q: What advice would you give women navigating work-life balance?
A: It's essential to reject the notion of a perfect balance. It's about integration and priorities. There are times when work will take precedence and others when personal life needs to. It's a fluid dance, not a rigid schedule.

Interview 3: Emily Chiu, Executive Director at GreenFuture NGO

Q: In your experience, what challenges do women in leadership face in the NGO sector?

A: There's often a misconception that the NGO sector is less ruthless. However, funding battles and stakeholder management require assertive leadership. Women, too often seen as nurturing, have to work harder to be taken seriously in these aggressive arenas.

Q: How have you cultivated executive presence in a field often driven by compassion?

A: For me, it's been about harmonising compassion with command. I ensure my passion for the cause shines through but also that my team sees a leader with a clear vision and the determination to see it through.

Interview 4: Laura Smith, Founding Partner at Smith & Co. Law Firm

Q: Laura, you've built a successful firm in a traditional field. What's been your experience closing the gender pay gap?

A: Transparency has been key. We've instituted open conversations about salary and progression criteria, and we regularly benchmark our salaries. It's a commitment to fairness that's not just ethical but beneficial for the business.

Q: What's been your approach to decision-making?

A: My approach values both intuition and data. However, it's critical not to shy away from risks—they are often necessary for growth. Preparing thoroughly, then having the courage to leap, is how we've moved forward.

The enlightening dialogues presented here are mere snippets of the vast reservoir of wisdom shared by these commendable leaders. Each transcript herein is a testament to the courage, intellect, and empathy embodied by women who have risen to the pinnacle of leadership, offering valuable insights for those who aspire to walk in their footsteps. Their experiences form a blueprint of perseverance, adaptability, and strategic thinking that is instrumental in navigating the corporate realm as it evolves to embrace equitable representation at its helm.

www.ingramcontent.com/pod-product-compliance
Lightning Source LLC
Chambersburg PA
CBHW030005190526
45157CB00014B/441